DEC 2 8 2018

CULTURES OF THE WORLD

Mongolia

Cavendish Square
New York

Published in 2019 by Cavendish Square Publishing, LLC
243 5th Avenue, Suite 136, New York, NY 10016

Copyright © 2019 by Cavendish Square Publishing, LLC

Third Edition

No part of this publication may be reproduced, stored in a retrieval system, or transmitted in any form or by any means—electronic, mechanical, photocopying, recording, or otherwise—without the prior permission of the copyright owner. Request for permission should be addressed to Permissions, Cavendish Square Publishing, 243 5th Avenue, Suite 136, New York, NY 10016. Tel (877) 980-4450; fax (877) 980-4454.

Website: cavendishsq.com

This publication represents the opinions and views of the author based on his or her personal experience, knowledge, and research. The information in this book serves as a general guide only. The author and publisher have used their best efforts in preparing this book and disclaim liability rising directly or indirectly from the use and application of this book.

All websites were available and accurate when this book was sent to press.

Library of Congress Cataloging-in-Publication Data

Names: Toth, Henrietta, author. | Pang, Guek-Cheng, 1950-
Title: Mongolia / Henrietta Toth and Pang Guek Cheng.
Description: First edition. | New York : Cavendish Square, [2019] |
Series: Cultures of the world | Includes bibliographical references and index.
Identifiers: LCCN 2018024817 (print) | LCCN 2018031637 (ebook) |
ISBN 9781502641304 (ebook) | ISBN 9781502641298 (library bound) |
Subjects: LCSH: Mongolia--Juvenile literature.
Classification: LCC DS798 (ebook) | LCC DS798 .P34 2019 (print) | DDC 951.7/3--dc23
LC record available at https://lccn.loc.gov/2018024817

Editorial Director: David McNamara
Editor: Elizabeth Schmermund
Copy Editor: Nathan Heidelberger
Associate Art Director: Alan Sliwinski
Designer: Jessica Nevins
Production Coordinator: Karol Szymczuk
Photo Research: J8 Media

The photographs in this book are used by permission and through the courtesy of: cover Tuul and Bruno Morandi/Alamy Stock Photo; p. 1 Son of Sun/Shutterstock.com; p. 3 Valerii M/Shutterstock.com; p. 5, 6, 77, 91 Jakub Czajkowski/Shutterstock.com; p. 7 Toiletroom/Shutterstock.com; p. 8 Hecke61/Shutterstock.com; p. 10 Photowind/Shutterstock.com; p. 12 Chester Voyage/Alamy Stock Photo; p. 13 Anton Petrus/Shutterstock.com; p. 15 Chantal de Bruijne/Shutterstock.com; p. 16 Humannet/Shutterstock.com; p. 19 Saiko3p/Shutterstock.com; p. 20 Camilkuo/Shutterstock.com; p. 23 DeAgostini/Getty Images; p. 24 Peter Hermes Furian/Shutterstock.com; p. 27 File:Ungernsternbergr.jpg/Wikimedia Commons/Public Domain; p. 28 File:Tserendorj Signs Pact 1921.jpg/Wikimedia Commons/File:Tserendorj Signs Pact 1921.jpg/Public Domain; p. 29 Wikimedia Commons/File:Sukhbaatar and Choibalsan.jpg/Public Domain; p. 30 soviet reporter/Wikimedia Commons/File:Khalkhin Gol George Zhukov and Khorloogiin Choibalsan 1939 - 2.jpg; p. 31 Kremlin.ru (http://www.kremlin.ru)/Wikimedia Commons/File:Tsakhiagiin Elbegdorj, BRICSsummit 2015.jpg/CC BY 4.0; p. 32 Nomuun/Wikimedia Commons/File:The Plenary session hall of the StateGreat Hural.JPG/CC BY SA 3.0; p. 36, 92 Fred DuFour/AFP/Getty Images; p. 38 U.S. Air Force photo/Senior Airman Steele C. G. Britton/Wikimedia Commons/File:Mongolian Army soldiers salute while theirnation's flag waves in the breeze at the TransitCenter at Manas.jpg/Public Domain; p. 40 Tomohiro Ohsumi/Bloomberg/Getty Images; p. 42 Taylor Weidman/Bloomberg/Getty Images; p. 43 Dmitry Pichugin/Shutterstock.com; p. 44 Brent Lewin/Bloomberg/Getty Images; p. 45, 88 Thomas Koehler/Photothek/Getty Images; p. 46 (top) Joel Saget/AFP/Getty Images, (bottom) Chinneeb/Wikimedia Commons/File:ULN Airport.jpg/CC BT SA 3.0; p. 47 Education Images/UIG via Getty Images; p. 48 Christopher Meder/Shutterstock.com; p. 50 Fedor Selivanov/Shutterstock.com; p. 51 Jacques Langevin/Sygma/Getty Images; p. 52 SeongJoon Cho/Bloomber/ Getty Images; p. 53 Shoyuramen/Wikimedia Commons/File:Russian style building.JPG/CC BY SA 3.0; p. 54 Ganzorig Miimaa/Shutterstock.com; p. 56 Galyna Andrushko/Shutterstock.com; p. 57 China Photos/Getty Images; p. 59 JonasGratzer/LightRocket/Getty Images; p. 60 Michael Karavanov/Wikimedia Commons/File:Hovsgol Lake at sunset panoramio.Jpg/CC BY SA 3.0; p. 61 DeAgostini/Getty Images; p. 62 Katiekk/Shutterstock.com; p. 63 Vidor at English Wikipedia/Wikimedia Commons/File:Gorkhi Terelj Park.jpg/Public Domain; p. 64 Igor Ageenko/Shutterstock.com; p. 66 Three Lions/Hulton Archive/Getty Images; p. 68 Kyodo News/Getty Images; p. 69 Aleksander Hunta/Shutterstock.com; p. 70 Yavuz Sariyildiz/Shutterstock.com; p. 72 Yavuz Sariyildiz/Shutterstock.com; p. 73 Wikimedia Commons/File:Natsagdorj.jpg/Public Doimain; p. 74 Hadynyah/iStockphoto.com; p. 76 Chanwit Whanset/Shutterstock.com; p. 78 (top), 80 (top) Dmitry Chulov/Shutterstock.com, (bottom) Dinozzzave/Shutterstock.com; p. 79 Pierre Jean Durieu/Shutterstock.com; p. 80 (bottom) Pauline Taylor/Alamy Stock Photo; p. 82 Orgio89/Wikimedia Commons/File:Mongolian National University.jpg/CC BY SA 3.0; p. 84 Peter Zachar/Shutterstock.com; p. 86 Manan Vatsysyana/AFP/Getty Images; p.87 Beibaoke/Shutterstock.com; p. 89 Elena Kitch/Shutterstock.com; p. 95 Simeon DonoviStockphoto.com; p. 96 Gil C/Shutterstock.com; p. 97 Gantuya eng at English Wikipedia/Wikimedia Commons/File:MongolianScripts.JPG/Public Domain; p. 98 Saul Loeb/AFP/Getty Images; p. 100 Mark Heard/Wikimedia Commons/File:Kazakh rug chain stitch embroidery.jpg/CC BY SA 2.0; p. 102, 112 TaylorWeidman/LightRocket/Getty Images; p. 103 Tina Manley/Alamy Stock Photo; p. 104 Katoosha/Shutterstock.com; p. 105 (top) 105 David Berkowitz/Wikimedia Commons/File:Danzanravjaa Museum of Sainshand-1.jpg/CC BY 2.0, (bottom) Gyula Péter/Wikimedia Commons/File:Séta Karakorum romjai között (Walking at theruins of Kharakhorum) panoramio.Jpg/CC BY SA 3.0; p. 106 Mechanical Curator collection/The British Library/Wikimedia Commons/File:KARMANSIN(1828) p1.387 Schriftproben.jpg/Public Domain; p. 107, 109 Wolfgang Kaehler/LightRocket/Getty Images; p. 110 Thomas Trutschel/Photothek/Getty Images; p. 113 (top) Mark Fischer/Wikimedia Commons/File:Nadaam Racers.jpg/CC BY SA 2.0, (bottom) EmmePi Stock Images/Alamy Stock Photo; p. 114 Miguel Angel Bastida/Wikimedia Commons/File:Deer Mx at Baotou.jpg/CC BY SA 4.0; p. 115 Alexander Hassenstein/Getty Images; p. 116 Look and Learn/Bridgeman Images; p. 118 Katiekk/Shutterstock.com; p. 120 Donikz/Shutterstock.com; p. 121 (top) Chanwit Whanset/Shutterstock.com, (bottom) Chinneeb/Wikimedia Commons/File:Naadam2014Archery.JPG/CC BY SA 4.0; p. 122 Michel Setboun/Corbis/Getty Images; p. 124 De Visu/Shutterstock.com; p. 126 Marco Giovanelli/Barcroft Media/Getty Images; p. 128 Anthony Asael/Art in All of Us/Getty Images; p. 129 Richard Manning/Getty Images; p. 130 Mizu Basyo/Wikimedia Commons/File:Guriltai shul.jpg/CC BY SA 1.0; p. 131 https://www.flickr.com/photos/davidberkowitz/Wikimedia Commons/File:Mutton Pancakes at Mongolian'sRestaurant & Pub.jpg/CC BY SA 2.0.

Printed in the United States of America

CONTENTS

MONGOLIA TODAY 5

1. GEOGRAPHY
Mountains and forests • An ancient desert • The grasslands • Sources of water • A continental climate • Land of wind and blue sky • Unique animal life • Towns and cities **11**

2. HISTORY
A people on the move • An empire rises • The empire expands • The end of the empire • Inner and Outer Mongolia • Shifts in government • Life under communism • The move toward democracy **21**

3. GOVERNMENT
Central government • Local government • Government unrest • A new constitution • The military • International diplomacy **33**

4. ECONOMY
A changing economy • Livestock and crops • Harvesting timber and fish • Harvesting coal and minerals • Fuel and electricity • Manufacturing • Building and plants • Modes of transport • Information technology • Financial institutions • Imports and exports • Labor force • Travel to Mongolia • Investing in business • Supply and demand **41**

5. ENVIRONMENT
A delicate ecosystem • A push to advancement • Overtaxing the land • A polluted environment • An environmental plan • Protecting the land and animals **55**

6. MONGOLIANS
The ethnicity of Mongolia • An ancient social system • A reorganized society • Traditional Mongolian clothes **67**

7. LIFESTYLE
An old way of life made new • Necessary livestock • The nomad's house • Mongolian women today • Marriage in Mongolia • Modern and traditional medicine • Educational opportunities **75**

8. RELIGION
Mongolia's early religion • The return of the monastery • The spirit world • Myths and superstitions • Other religions **85**

9. LANGUAGE
Speaking Mongolian • Writing Mongolian • The press and broadcasting • Names and titles • Unspoken communication **93**

10. ARTS
Early material culture • Art in Mongolia • Written works • Physical structures • Arts and crafts • Music in Mongolia **101**

11. LEISURE
Athletic competitions • Ancient pastimes • The pursuit of game • Leisure-time activities • Athletic games • Traditional stories **111**

12. FESTIVALS
Celebrating the new year • A big festival • A religious festival • A child's first haircut **119**

13. FOOD
A mostly meat diet • Milk products • A pot of tea **125**

MAP OF MONGOLIA **133**

ABOUT THE ECONOMY **135**

ABOUT THE CULTURE **137**

TIMELINE **138**

GLOSSARY **140**

FOR FURTHER INFORMATION **141**

BIBLIOGRAPHY **142**

INDEX **143**

MONGOLIA TODAY

MONGOLIA IS A LAND OF STRIKING CONTRASTS. IT IS A COUNTRY with an ancient history and deeply rooted way of life balancing the changes brought on by modern ways and a quickly evolving future. Mongolia is perhaps best known for dominating the history of the thirteenth century when fierce warriors galloped across central Asia in bloody invasions to carve out the Mongol Empire. The skillful horsemen of the Mongol army could shoot arrows at long range while at a wild gallop. Mongolia is known for Genghis Khan, ruler of the empire beginning in 1206; and it is known for Marco Polo and the amazing tales he brought back from the court of Kublai Khan. The great Mongol Empire developed from the unification of nomadic tribes who herded their animals to better pastures and picked up their homes when they were on the move. It was a simple yet hard way of life that is still prevalent, although the nomadic existence is changing. This nation that once seemed cut off from the modern world is embracing some of the new ways that come with it.

Located in northern Asia, Mongolia is wedged between the two larger and more powerful nations of China and Russia. It is the eighteenth-largest country on earth, with a total landmass of more than 600,000 square miles (1.5 million square kilometers).

The land in Mongolia varies from deserts to grasslands to mountains.

It has an extremely varied geography of deserts, grasslands, and mountains. The high mountain ranges, which contain some extinct volcanoes, are popular with climbers. Parts of the landscape are harsh deserts like the Gobi, which is partly in China. The Great Gobi is Asia's largest and the world's fifth-biggest desert. Its sands have yielded dinosaur fossils from one hundred million years ago. In eastern Mongolia are the steppes, or grasslands, that feed the country's livestock and make up a major portion of the economy. The Asian camels and Mongolian horses are animals distinctive to Mongolia. The country is landlocked and dry with little rainfall, making its rivers and lakes all the more important. Most Mongolians live in small towns, and many still call the traditional housing of a *ger* home. There are also larger cities like the capital, Ulaanbaatar, which is developing into a modern metropolis and contrasts greatly with nomadic life. One-third of Mongolia's population of three million lives in Ulaanbaatar. That makes the rest of the country one of the most sparsely populated nations, with just an average of 4.3 people per square mile (2.6 per sq km).

Mongolia's growing population has taken a toll on the land.

Thirty percent of the people are nomads who herd more than fifty million animals. They represent the last nomadic way of life in the world.

For centuries, Mongolia was a feudal society. It became a socialist state in the early twentieth century under Russian influence. Toward the turn of the twenty-first century, Mongolia became a developing and democratic country, establishing trade and foreign relations with other nations. Since 1990, Mongolia has had a multiparty parliamentary government that maintains diplomatic relations with more than 160 nations. Mongolia's economy has mirrored the changes in its government. It had a traditional economy before a socialist system took its place during the communist era. A market economy emerged in the later 1980s moving into an open-market system. In addition to the traditional raising of livestock, Mongolia's economy has been boosted by forestry, construction and industry, communications and transportation, and tourism. However, two resources in particular dominate the economy: mining and textiles. The tenth-largest mining reserves in the world are in

A colossal statue of Genghis Khan looms over the steppes of Mongolia.

Mongolia, and the country is second only behind China in the production of goat-wool cashmere. Overall economic growth has picked up after a slowdown of several years, but the poverty rate is still high, especially in rural areas.

Mongolia's emergence into the modern world has taken a toll on its environment. Traditionally, Mongolian nomads have lived as the land and the climate allowed. The push for progress has caused soil erosion, deforestation, and poor wildlife management. The growing population of the country has been affected by water and air pollution. UNICEF has called for action to the air pollution crisis on behalf of Mongolia's children, while the government promises to enact more measures.

Tibetan Buddhism is the main religion of Mongolia, with more than half of the population practicing the faith that was introduced in the sixteenth century. Ancient rituals of shamanism to connect to the spirit world and nature are also practiced. And once again monasteries are taking their place on the landscape of the country after many were destroyed during communist rule.

For fun and leisure, Mongolians enjoy a good festival, and Naadam is the largest one in the country. Although it lost its religious significance during communism, the festival takes place every year from July 11 to 13. The whole country celebrates at the same time, from small towns to the largest celebration held in Ulaanbaatar. There are parades of traditional costumes, music concerts, and Mongolian foods like mare's milk, meat kebabs, and the customary *khuushuur*—a fried dough pocket filled with beef or mutton. However, it is the athletic competitions that take center stage. Naadam is like an Olympic competition that pays homage to the warrior skills of centuries past with archery, horse racing, and wrestling. Thousands of wrestlers and thousands of horses and riders compete.

In fact, Mongolia is horse country, and there are more horses than people in the nation. Even the largest equestrian statue in the world is in Mongolia, that of Genghis Khan on horseback. It commemorates the conqueror and ruler of the largest empire in history and is located 34 miles (54 kilometers) from metropolitan Ulaanbaatar. The stainless steel statue is 130 feet (40 meters) tall, weighs 250 tons (226 metric tons), and sits atop a visitor center. It was completed in 2008.

Mongolia is a country where the old ways continue to meet the new ones. However, its rich and historic culture is not forgotten in the midst of embracing progress and the future. After moving past the effects of six decades of communist rule, Mongolia is finding its footing in the modern world while honoring its traditions.

GEOGRAPHY

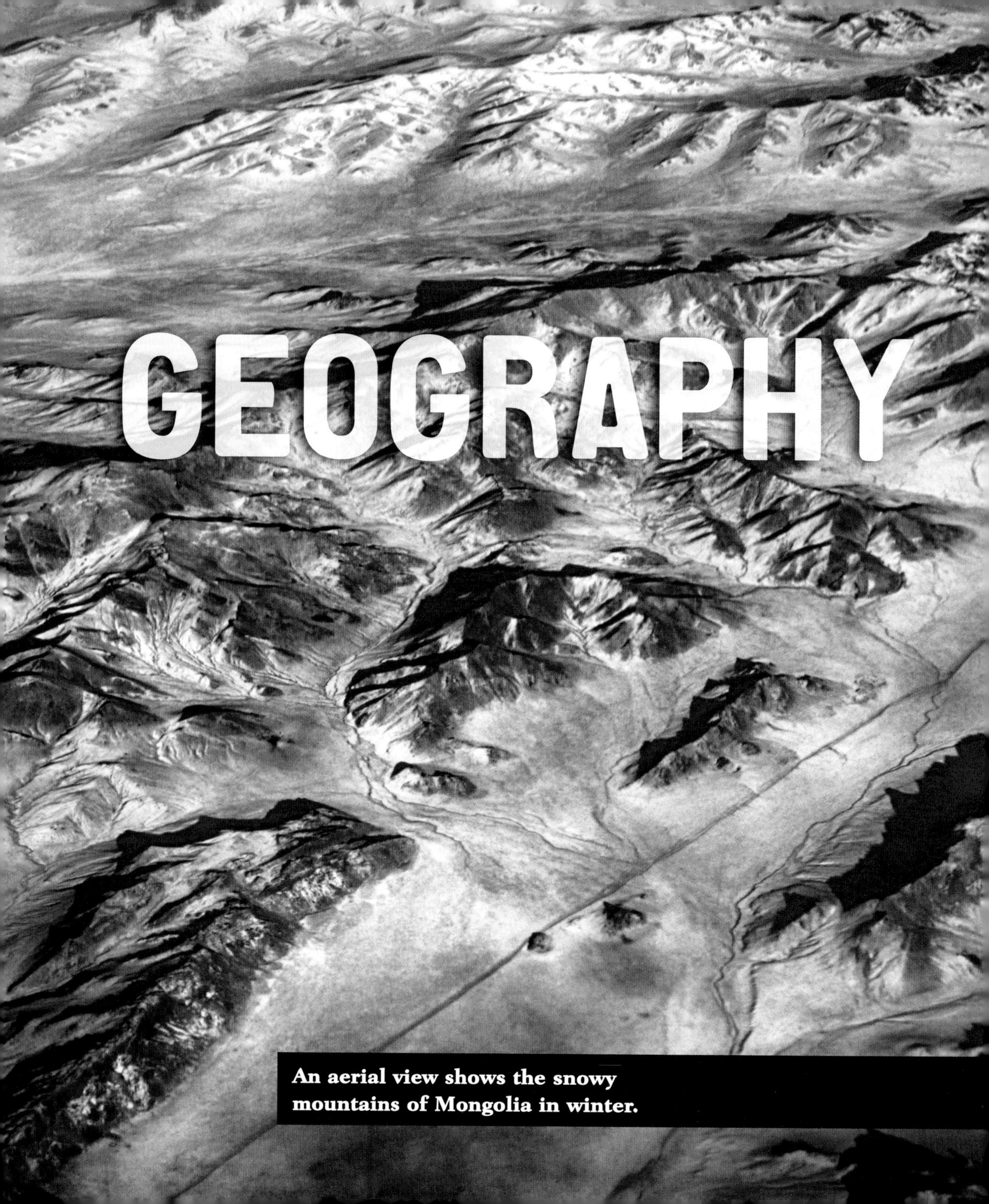

An aerial view shows the snowy mountains of Mongolia in winter.

1

THE RUGGED, OVAL-SHAPED LANDS of Mongolia lie in northern Asia. They are sandwiched between the larger and more powerful countries of Russia and China. In the north, Mongolia is bordered by the Russian province of Siberia for more than 2,140 miles (3,450 km). In the south, Mongolia shares a 2,875-mile (4,630 km) border with China. Mongolia is an independent country sometimes referred to as Outer Mongolia. It is separate from Inner Mongolia, an autonomous region in northern China. Mongolia encompasses 604,000 square miles (1,564,000 sq km), making it slightly smaller than Alaska and twice the size of Texas. Its population is a little more than three million and is concentrated in the northern capital city of Ulaanbaatar, home to more than one million people.

"From the air Mongolia looks like God's preliminary sketch for earth, not so much a country as the ingredients out of which countries are made: grass, rock, water and wind."

—Stanley Stewart, *In the Empire of Genghis Khan*

Hikers cross a high pass in the Altai Mountains.

MOUNTAINS AND FORESTS

Mongolia has a high average altitude of 5,013 feet (1,528 m) above sea level, though mountainous areas higher than 12,000 feet (3,658 m) form less than 5 percent of the total land area. About 40 percent of the country lies between 3,000 feet (914 m) and 10,000 feet (3,048 m) above sea level. Even the lowest part, the Hoh Nuur depression in the east, is 1,837 feet (560 m) above sea level. The higher areas are in western, northern, and central Mongolia, and the lower elevations are in the east and south.

There are three major mountain ranges in Mongolia: the Altai, the Khangai, and the Khentii. The Altai range in the west and southwest is the largest and highest range in the country. The highest point is the Khuiten Peak (Nayramadlin Orgil), which rises to 14,350 feet (4,374 m) above sea level, in the Tavan Bogd Uul mountain group of the Altai range. Much of this range is snow-covered all year round.

The predominantly forested Khangai and Khentii ranges are located in the north-central and northwestern parts of Mongolia. The mountain slopes of these ranges are wooded with cedar, larch, birch, pine, and fir. Above the timberline are alpine meadows with mosses and lichens that bloom in the spring. On the northern part of the Khangai Mountains are several extinct volcanoes and volcanic crater lakes. Wild sheep, ibex, and gazelles roam the mountains. The endangered snow leopard inhabits the high mountains along the border with Russia.

Mountaineers from all over the world visit Mongolia to climb the mountains, especially the Altai range. The short mountain-climbing season begins in early July and ends in August.

ONE GIANT STEP

The Gobi Desert has yielded one of the largest dinosaur footprints ever unearthed. Measuring 4 feet (1.2 m) long, the well-preserved fossil footprint includes an impression of the dinosaur's claws. A team of archaeologists from Mongolia and Japan discovered the footprint in a geological layer that is between seventy and ninety million years old. This important find could give clues as to how the enormous titanosaur walked.

AN ANCIENT DESERT

In the south-central part of the country lies the famous Gobi Desert, which Mongolia shares with China. The largest desert in Asia, the Gobi is also known as Shamo, which means sand in Chinese. The Gobi is the world's coldest, northernmost desert, covering more than 500,000 square miles (1.3 million sq km). Windswept and nearly treeless, only 5 percent of it is sand dunes, while the rest is mostly dry, rocky, and sandy soil. The Gobi is actually a plateau of

Sand dunes ripple across the Gobi Desert.

DIGGING FOR DINOSAURS

When naturalist, adventurer, and fossil hunter Roy Chapman Andrews (1884–1960) drove across the Gobi Desert in 1918, he thought he had found the Garden of Eden. Andrews worked at the American Museum of Natural History in New York City, where he was its director from 1935 to 1942. During the 1920s, he returned to the Gobi, leading a scientific expedition for the museum. He had hoped to find the bones of early humans to confirm a theory that Homo sapiens *had evolved in high, dry climates like those of central Asia. Instead, he found that the Gobi was a vast repository of dinosaur remains. Andrews discovered the first dinosaur eggs when scientists were not sure that dinosaurs laid eggs. The eggs were found in the part of the Gobi known as Ulan Usu, which Andrews called the "Flaming Red Cliffs" because its cliffs, buttes, and gullies are made of red rock.*

Other expeditions to the Gobi have discovered fossilized animals and plants from the early Paleozoic and Mesozoic eras, when this area was covered by great seas and lakes. The Gobi has yielded the skeletons of previously unknown dinosaurs, as well as the tiny skulls of some of the earliest identified mammals. The desert fossil beds are extensive and well preserved because of the dry desert climate.

In the 1960s, a Mongolian-Polish scientific team discovered the skeletons of a velociraptor and a protoceratops that died during a violent sandstorm that swept over them as they tried to kill each other. In 1993, a team from the American Museum of Natural History and the Mongolian Academy of Sciences discovered an oviraptor fossil seated on a clutch of eggs—the first evidence of a dinosaur showing parental care.

"We realized we were looking at the first dinosaur eggs ever seen by a human being … The elongated shape of the eggs was distinctly reptilian."
—Roy Chapman Andrews, *On the Trail of Ancient Man*

rolling gravel plains with occasional low ranges and isolated hills. It rises from 3,000 feet (914 m) in the east to 5,000 feet (1,524 m) in the west, where it meets the Altai Mountains. The desert vegetation is grass and scrub. People and livestock living there rely on water from small, shallow lakes and wells.

Caravan routes have crisscrossed the Gobi since ancient times. In about 1275, Marco Polo, along with his father and his uncle, were the first Europeans to cross the desert. The Gobi is a famous repository of fossils, especially specimens from the Late Cretaceous period from one hundred million years ago.

The river valley and steppes of Karakorum have an ancient history.

THE GRASSLANDS

The steppes, or grasslands, mainly cover the eastern part of the country. The vegetation consists of varieties of feather grass common to the steppes of central Asia. These grasses sustain the millions of sheep, horses, goats, cattle, and other livestock that graze there and are the mainstay of the Mongolian economy. Herds of antelope also roam the grasslands.

In the springtime, the harsh look that the countryside wears through most of the year changes. It slowly turns a vivid green as everything comes alive with some hills carpeted in a tapestry of bright yellow, purple, pale violet, and crimson. Millions of wildflowers burst into bloom to make the most of their short growing season.

SOURCES OF WATER

Mongolia is a dry land. Average total rainfall during the year is below 8 inches (200 millimeters) in the desert and 12 inches (300 mm) in the north. Thus, the

Lakes in Mongolia have been shrinking.

many rivers, lakes, and glaciers are important sources of water.

Over 1,200 rivers flow in three distinct directions—north into the Arctic Ocean, east into the Pacific Ocean, and south into the desert. Mongolia's main rivers include the Selenge, one of the rivers flowing into Lake Baikal in Russia; the Orkhon, a tributary of the Selenge; and the Tuul. The source of all three rivers is in the Khangai range. The Kherlen River originates in the Khentii range. A vital resource of water for years to come, there are about two hundred glaciers in the Altai Mountains alone.

Mongolia has more than four thousand lakes. Many are small, with an average surface area of 2 square miles (5 sq km), but the total area of all the lakes is just over 1 percent of Mongolia's land area. Many lakes were formed by glacial and volcanic activity and are concentrated between the Altai and the Khangai ranges.

A CONTINENTAL CLIMATE

Mongolia lies around latitude 46°N and longitude 105°E, in the same belt as Ukraine, Romania, Hungary, Austria, and the northern United States. The country is completely landlocked. The nearest water is the Yellow Sea, about 435 miles (700 km) beyond the eastern border.

Mongolia has a continental climate characterized by extreme temperature changes. From November to March, average temperatures are below freezing. The coldest month is usually January, when temperatures can drop to as low as −9 degrees Fahrenheit (−23 degrees Celsius). In the summer, the hottest month is usually July, when temperatures range from 68°F (20°C) in the northern regions to about 50°F–80°F (10°C–27°C) in the south. Temperature changes of as many degrees as 35°F–55°F (19°C–31°C) can occur in one day.

LAND OF WIND AND BLUE SKY

The distance from the sea and the fact that any moisture-laden winds from the east encounter a mountain range ensure that the winds that blow over Mongolia are dry. Mongolia has very little rainfall, although the mountainous regions of the north are wetter than the southern parts. The rainy season is between May and September.

The lack of humidity means that on most days the sun shines brightly from a blue and often cloudless sky. Mongolians boast that they can bask in as many as 250 sunny days a year. Traditional Mongolians believe the immense blue sky is the supreme god called Tengri (TENG-ri). For Mongolians, blue is a lucky color, and it is incorporated in their national emblem.

Mongolia is also known as the land of winds because of the sharp gusts that blow in the springtime and often turn into storms.

UNIQUE ANIMAL LIFE

The Asian, or Bactrian, camels of Mongolia are critically endangered, with less than one thousand remaining in the wild in the southwest part of the country and in the northwest of China. These camels have two humps and are smaller than the Arabian camel, or dromedary. They graze on the sparse desert grasses and can live for three months on water alone.

The Mongolian horse is small, with a thick, well-muscled neck and a very bulky head. It is remarkably tough and can easily survive harsh winters. It resembles the Przewalski's horse, a rare species of wild horse that once roamed the Gobi Desert and the steppes in great numbers and that has narrowly avoided extinction. Unlike the more common domesticated breeds, Przewalski's horses are nearly impossible to tame.

Mongolia is a resting point for migratory birds that fly from the northern parts of the Asian continent to the warmer shores of the Indian and Pacific Oceans in the winter. These are mainly waterfowl and other birds that live near water.

"The real summer lasts only from May till August. Then, the valleys are like an exquisite garden and the woods are ablaze with color. Bluebells, their stalks bending under the weight of blossoms, clothe every hillside in a glorious azure dress bespangled with yellow roses, daisies, and forget-me-nots."
—Roy Chapman Andrews, *Across Mongolian Plains*

CHALLENGED BY GEOGRAPHY

Mongolia is landlocked and isolated by its unique geographic features of plateaus, mountains, grasslands, and desert. The steppes, or grasslands, are one of the country's best-known regions. In the thirteenth century, Mongol horse warriors fanned out across the steppes to gain control of other agricultural communities. Now agriculture makes up less than 15 percent of Mongolia's economy. Larger efforts are in mining the country's vast deposits of coal, copper, gold, and uranium. However, this has made Mongolia dependent on the capital and expertise of foreign investors. Plus, as a land without deepwater ports it must depend on its neighbors, China and Russia, to export these resources. Mongolia's isolation between these two stronger nations makes it hard to bargain with a third country and offset the influence of its neighbors.

TOWNS AND CITIES

Many Mongolians live in the countryside in small towns. The facilities in such towns usually include concrete municipal office buildings, a central square, a dilapidated power station, and a reserve fuel dump on the outskirts to supply the trucks passing by. Residents live in concrete apartment buildings or in gers, also called yurts—traditional structures made of a wooden frame covered with layers of felt. A wooden fence surrounds each ger so that it can be assigned a house number. The town administration provides the residents with postal and other services. Sometimes there are also communities of several hundred gers laid out in blocks separated by roads.

The capital city, Ulaanbaatar, earlier known as Urga, was founded in 1639. Its name changed many times before becoming Ulaanbaatar ("Red Hero") in 1924. The settlement was once a center of Buddhism and the residence of the Bogd Khan, a religious leader. The city of nearly 1.4 million (2015 estimate) lies in the Tuul River valley of north-central Mongolia. It is the political, cultural, economic, and industrial center of the country and the only big city in terms of population. About one-third of the entire Mongolian population lives in modern Ulaanbaatar.

Erdenet has the second-largest population, almost 80,000, and lies in the north between the Selenge and Orkhon Rivers. The town grew around an ore-processing plant that was built in 1973. This plant is one of the largest in Asia, producing approximately 530,000 tons (480,800 metric tons) of copper concentrate annually.

Darkhan, north of the capital, is the third-largest city, with about 74,300 residents. It is an industrial center built from the ground up in 1961 in an area rich in limestone, sand, clay, marble, and coal—materials important in construction. Darkhan is the hub of the construction industry and also produces consumer goods and foodstuffs.

Crowds gather on Chinggis Square in Ulaanbaatar for the annual Naadam festival.

INTERNET LINKS

https://earthobservatory.nasa.gov/NaturalHazards/view.php?id=79746
The Earth Observatory website has images of dust storms in the Gobi Desert taken by a NASA satellite.

https://www.youtube.com/watch?v=FBFGLm5HwXY
In this National Geographic video, explorer Tim Cope retraces the 6,000-mile (9,650 km) route traveled by conqueror Genghis Khan.

HISTORY

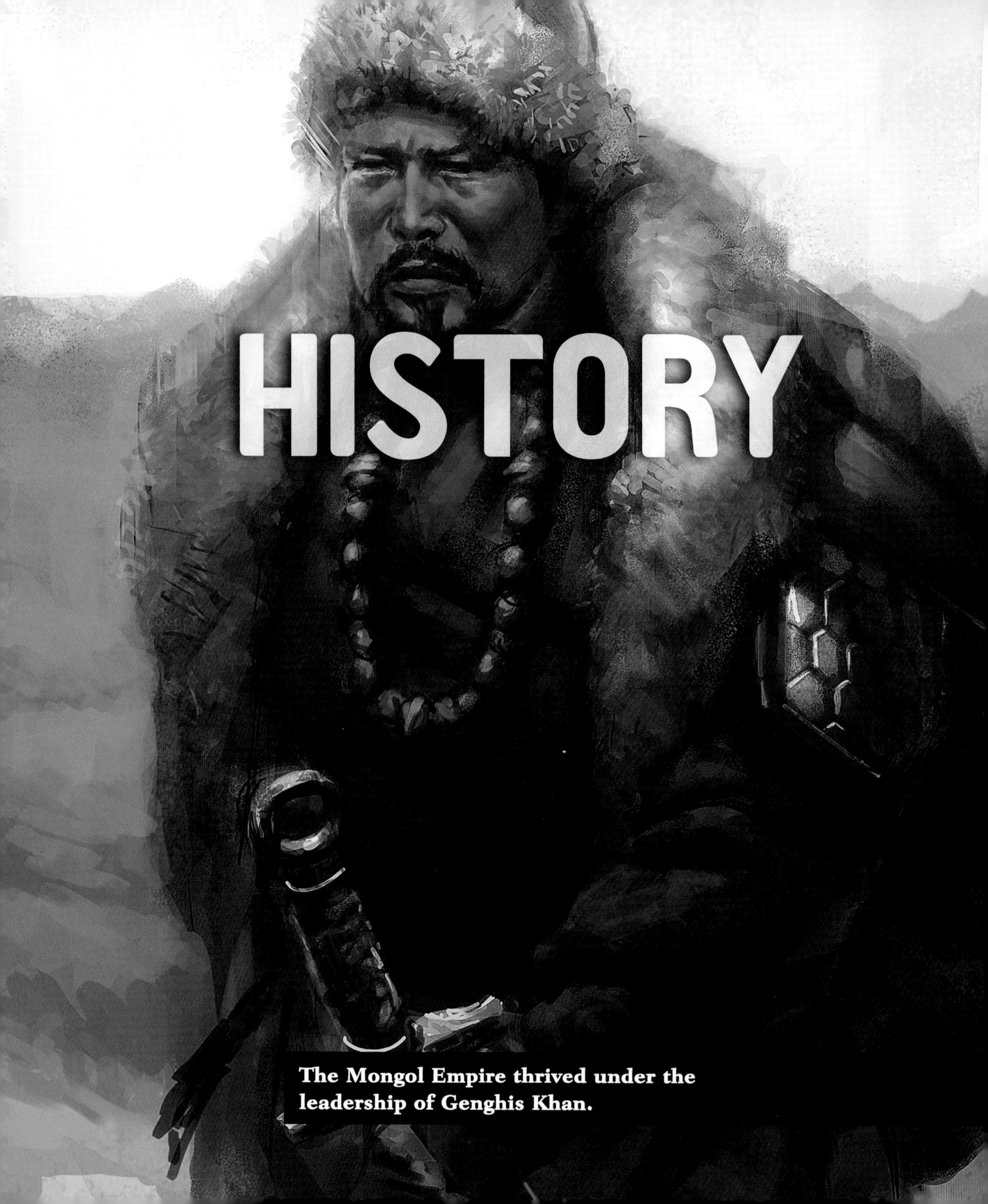

The Mongol Empire thrived under the leadership of Genghis Khan.

2

MONGOLIA HAS A COLORFUL AND rich history that spans centuries and many lands. In the thirteenth century, the Mongol warriors were feared as they rode forcefully into the heart of Asia. The Mongols subjugated all the nations from central Asia to the banks of the Danube River in central Europe. These conquered lands were forged into a large and fierce empire under the famed ruler Genghis Khan and his descendants. The Mongols dominated China for more than a century and Russia for more than two centuries before the decline of the empire. Mongolia's more recent history has been shaped by political turmoil and government upheavals, moving it from an empire to a communist state to a democracy.

"Those who were adept and brave fellows I have made military commanders. Those who were quick and nimble I have made herders of horses. Those who were not adept I have given a small whip and sent to be shepherds."

—Genghis Khan

A PEOPLE ON THE MOVE

The steppes of central Asia were inhabited by nomadic tribes—probably of Turkic, Tataric, or Ugrian origin—before the Mongolian nation emerged. The Chinese emperor Shi Huang Di built the first part of the Great Wall of China to keep out these marauding tribes, specifically the Xiongnu, believed to be related to the Huns, another fierce band of conquerors. The famous tomb of Shi Huang Di contains over six thousand life-size terra-cotta figures of soldiers and horses.

In 209 BCE, the Huns established the first state in central Asia. The Huns later split into two groups. One went west, moving from the steppes north of the Caspian Sea to the Roman Empire during the fourth and fifth centuries CE. The other group entered the Han and Xia lands south of the Great Wall.

From the seventh to the tenth centuries, nomadic peoples—including the Avars, Turks, Uyghur, and Kitan—successively rose to power, became fragmented, and moved westward, or came to be integrated with the Chinese.

The Mongols were a small group of such nomadic people who moved from pasture to pasture with the seasons. They fought with each other and formed alliances when defeated in battle or when it was in their best interests to do so. These alliances would change according to the shifting strengths of the different clans.

The rise of the Mongol people began in the time of Chinggis Khan (1162–1227), commonly known as Genghis Khan. He was the first ruler of Mongolia to unite the tribes of central Asia. Before he became ruler, his name was Temujin. He inherited the leadership of his clan from his father and gained greater power by conquering or forging alliances with the other clans.

In 1206, at a great assembly of all the tribes, Temujin was proclaimed Genghis Khan, meaning "strong ruler," and all the clans agreed to adopt the name Mongol.

AN EMPIRE RISES

Genghis Khan began building his empire in 1209 with a campaign against the southern kingdom of Xi Xia, ruled by the Tanguts, who controlled the vital oases

THE MONGOL WAR MACHINE

The Mongol cavalryman was lightly armored in comparison to the European knight of antiquity. He was clad in leather armor, which gave him greater agility than metal armor. He carried a small leather shield on his left arm for protection. His weapons included a lance, a bow with a quiver of arrows, a saber, and a dagger. He had arrows that served different purposes. Some arrows had heads designed solely for killing that whistled when released to terrify the enemy, and others that whistled but only wounded the enemy. The Mongol bowman was trained to shoot while riding at a full gallop and was equally adept at hitting targets in front of him as well as behind him.

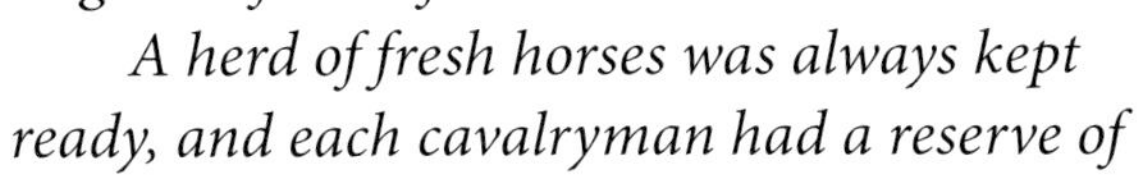

A herd of fresh horses was always kept ready, and each cavalryman had a reserve of up to four remounts. As part of their basic training, soldiers joined an annual game hunt in which wild animals were chased into a given area and shot by horsemen. Each soldier was given just one arrow to kill the animal of his choice.

Artillerymen with mangonels, or giant catapults, supported the cavalry. When laying siege to a town, the Mongols used these to hurl stones, rocks, trees, and even animal corpses to breach the walls.

along the Silk Road linking China with Rome. Caravans, including those of the Mongols, traveled the route carrying all kinds of goods and were heavily taxed by the Tanguts. Defeated in 1210, Xi Xia became Mongolia's first vassal state.

Next to be conquered was the Jin Empire, which was already struggling with internal troubles. Other conquests soon followed. The Mongols expanded west, defeating the Kara-Khitai Empire west of the Altai Mountains and the cities of Samarkand, Bukhara, Merv, and Herat, belonging to the Muslim empire of Khwarizm. The Mongols forged into Russian territory and threatened to

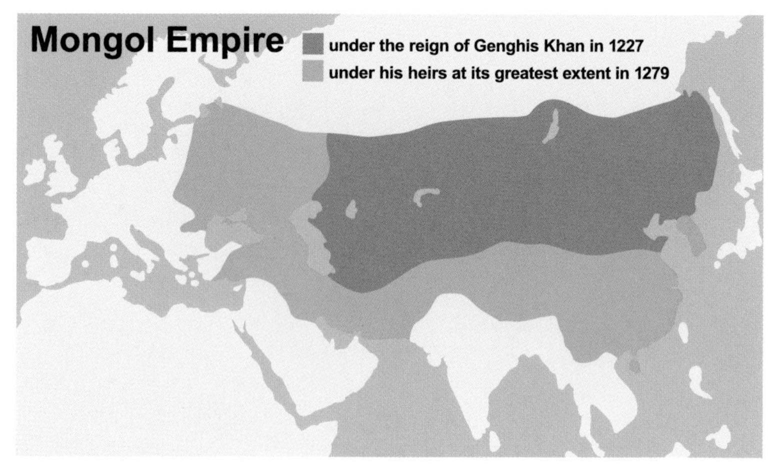

This map illustrates the size of the Mongol Empire.

conquer the Russian principalities of Kiev, Chernigov, Galicia, Rostov, and Suzdal, before deciding to return to their homeland in central Asia.

Many clans caught in the Mongol onslaught chose to submit rather than be killed. They paid taxes and provided men to the army, adding to the Mongol military strength. Chinese, Turks, Persians, Armenians, Georgians, and others fought alongside Mongol soldiers. Skilled craftsmen, musicians, scholars, and administrators were taken prisoner to serve the khan. Millions of people were subjugated. The wars of this period caused great destruction, but they also unified Asian and European tribes and for a very long time brought Eastern and Western civilizations face-to-face.

Genghis Khan died in 1227 from a fall off a horse. By 1280, the Mongol Empire built by Genghis, his sons Jochi, Chaghatai, Ogedei, and Tolui, and his grandsons stretched over all of Asia almost to the Mediterranean Sea. But the empire soon began to break down into smaller, independent fiefdoms ruled by different branches of the family.

THE EMPIRE EXPANDS

After Genghis died, his son Ogedei was chosen in 1229 to be the Great Khan. Ogedei continued to expand the empire. He subdued Xi Xia, which had rebelled, continued the efforts to annex the rich Song Empire, and sent a new army to the west. He made Karakorum his capital, transforming it from a simple base camp into a great walled city with the labor of captive skilled craftsmen. News of its splendors spread to the West. In 1238, the Mongols under Batu, Jochi's son, attacked and defeated Russia, a few principalities at a time, and moved on to Poland and Hungary in 1241. The Mongols then rode into Austria. When they had almost reached Vienna, news of Ogedei's death in 1241 arrived from Karakorum, and they withdrew. In the following years, there was a prolonged power struggle between Batu and his cousin Guyuk, Ogedei's son.

MILITARY FALL

The fall of the Mongols coincided with the progress made by the Manchus on their cannons and muskets—which the Mongols could not match. The Mongols were pushed by the Manchus to the north and the west, and by the Russians to the south and the east.

Batu remained in southern Russia, where he established his own capital, Sarai, and ruled his fiefdom, known as the Golden Horde. Power then passed to the sons of Tolui.

Mongke, Tolui's eldest son, was enthroned in 1251, and with his brother Kublai renewed the assault against the Song. Another brother, Hulegu, attacked Baghdad, the heart of the Muslim world. The caliph (ruler) and his family were massacred, and the Muslim empire became an Il-Khanate (subordinate khanate), ruled by Hulegu. His lands stretched from present-day Pakistan to Turkey. After Mongke died in 1259, a power struggle ensued between Kublai, still battling the Song, and Ariq Boke, the youngest brother, in Karakorum. Kublai returned to Mongolia and fought Ariq Boke, winning power in 1264. He proclaimed himself Great Khan. By this time, the powerful Mongol Empire had broken into fiefdoms.

Kublai spent much time in northern China (modern Inner Mongolia) and established a capital at Shangdu (often called Xanadu). He set himself the task of developing and unifying China. He founded the Yuan dynasty and moved his capital to the more centrally located Dadu (present-day Beijing). He encouraged trade, improved Chinese agriculture, advanced the study of the sciences, and developed a written script for the Mongolian language. In 1279, Kublai finally defeated the Song Empire and united north and south China. He attempted to invade Japan in 1274 and 1281, and Java in Southeast Asia in 1292, but without success. Kublai Khan died in 1294 at the age of seventy-nine.

The Mongols' eighty-nine-year rule of China, as the Yuan dynasty, ended in 1368, when the Chinese rebelled—tired of the ever-increasing taxes and the corruption of the officials. The Mongols were forced back to Mongolia by the succeeding Ming dynasty, whose rulers rebuilt the Great Wall of China to ensure that the Mongols and other marauding tribes were kept out for good.

THE END OF THE EMPIRE

After their defeat in China, the Mongols retreated to their homeland. Over the next few centuries, the unity that had bound together their great empire dissolved as the various clans jostled for power. Moreover, the Mongols were being squeezed between Russia and China. The Manchus—inhabitants of Manchuria—of northeast China had assumed power in China and formed the Qing dynasty (1644–1911). Russia and China had been making alliances, meanwhile, and rapidly expanding their influence in the area. From the fourteenth century until Mongolia became a people's republic in the early twentieth century, events in both Russia and China had a significant impact on Mongolia.

From the fourteenth to the seventeenth centuries, the Mongol tribes fought among themselves. The Oirats in the west split with the Khalkhas in the east. Eventually, these two remaining large groups splintered into smaller tribes that continued bickering among themselves, thus allowing the Chinese to invade and control them. The various fragmented tribes became the vassals of China.

In the late sixteenth century, Buddhism took hold in Mongolia. Gombordorji Zanabazar (1635–1723), the six-year-old young son of a wealthy prince, was proclaimed leader of the Buddhists in 1641. He was called the Javzandamba Khutagt, which means "reincarnate lama."

During the 1750s, the Manchus decided, for administrative purposes, to divide Mongolia into northern and southern regions. Known as Inner Mongolia, the southern provinces were essentially part of China. The northern provinces were called Outer Mongolia. Chinese traders and moneylenders played a defining role in Mongolian society. The Mongolians fell increasingly into debt to the Manchus, were forced to pay high taxes, and were resentful of being dominated by them. When the Manchus were overthrown in 1911 and the Republic of China was formed, Outer Mongolia, with Russia's support, took the opportunity to declare its independence.

INNER AND OUTER MONGOLIA

The Mongolian revolt was led by the eighth Javzandamba Khutagt, who ruled Mongolia with the consent of the Manchus. He was called the Bogd Khan, champion of God and supporter of civilization, and revered as a god-king, uniting state and religion. He backed Mongolian nationalistic ambitions with the aim of reuniting Mongolia once more. He even tried to reclaim the territory of Inner Mongolia from China. The god-king was also a drunkard and a womanizer who supported his decadent lifestyle by selling his blessings to the people.

In 1915, with Russian support, Mongolia was able to persuade China to sign a treaty involving all three countries. According to this treaty, Outer Mongolia was recognized as autonomous, although the Bogd Khan government was forced to accept Chinese suzerainty (meaning that China remained dominant in controlling Mongolian foreign affairs). But in 1919, Chinese troops invaded Mongolia and imprisoned the Bogd Khan. Russia, caught up in the upheaval of the Russian Revolution and World War I, was unable to help.

Baron Roman von Ungern-Sternberg posed for this photo in 1909.

Deliverance from the Chinese this time came through a strange and colorful figure, Baron Roman von Ungern-Sternberg, also known as the Mad Baron. He was a Russian czarist general who had escaped the revolution in Russia. He believed he was part of a divine plan to liberate Mongolia. In 1921, with an army of opportunists—which included Russians, Mongolians, Tibetans, and Poles—the baron attacked Urga, drove out the Chinese army, and rescued the Bogd Khan. Having helped Mongolia, the Mad Baron felt that the divine plan also called for him to save Russia from the communists—giving Russia an excuse to intervene in Mongolian affairs.

SHIFTS IN GOVERNMENT

Meanwhile, nationalistic feelings were on the rise in Mongolia. The people were increasingly opposed to the Chinese invaders as well as to the Mad Baron and his White Russian army, which was turning out to be an army of occupation. When the Chinese had invaded Mongolia in 1919, a group of Mongolian nationalists had fled across the border to Siberia, and in 1920 they

The Bogd Khan signs the independence treaty in 1921.

formed the Mongolian People's Party, later renamed the Mongolian People's Revolutionary Party (MPRP). Among them were the revolutionary leaders Damdiny Sukhbaatar and Khorloogiin Choibalsan.

When the Mad Baron drove out the Chinese occupiers in February 1921 and declared an independent Mongolia, the revolutionaries' task became twice as difficult. Mongolia had to be freed first from the Chinese and then from the White Russian army. But in March 1921, with the backing of socialist Russia, which in 1917 had undergone a revolution bringing down the czar, Sukhbaatar crossed the border and drove out both the Chinese and the White Russians and pushed on to capture Urga.

Independence was declared on July 11, 1921. The Bogd Khan was allowed to remain as head of state, making Mongolia a republican monarchy from 1921 to 1924. When he died in 1924, there was no attempt to find a successor. In 1924, Mongolia was declared the Mongolian People's Republic. Joseph Stalin's policies in the Soviet Union had far-reaching effects on Mongolia. There were campaigns of political terror, purges, arrests, and an attack against the Mongolian feudal culture. In 1929, when Stalin launched the policy of collectivization, Mongolia was expected to do the same. Hundreds of Russian advisers and technicians were brought in to help. This communist, Soviet-style republic with a one-party system remained in power until 1990.

"If we, all the people, are united in common effort and common will, there can be nothing in the world that we cannot achieve, that we will not have learned, or failed to do." —Damdiny Sukhbaatar, Mongolian national hero

LIFE UNDER COMMUNISM

Stalin's puppet in Mongolia was Marshal Khorloogiin Choibalsan. He was one of the founders of the Mongolian People's Revolutionary Party and controlled the government, army, and secret police. Mongolian livestock herders were divided into rich and poor. Anyone with more than two hundred sheep was considered rich, and his animals were seized and divided among the poor. Property was appropriated from the Buddhist monasteries. Thousands of lamas were killed outright, and hundreds of temples and monasteries were destroyed. Chinese businessmen and their families were expelled from the country.

DAMDINY SUKHBAATAR

Damdiny Sukhbaatar (1893–1923)—sukhbaatar *means "ax hero"—is regarded as Mongolia's greatest revolutionary hero. He was conscripted into the Mongolian army when he was nineteen. Intelligent and a natural leader, he soon became a junior noncommissioned officer (NCO). After distinguishing himself in border clashes with the Chinese, he was promoted to senior NCO.*

When the Chinese invaded Mongolia in 1919, he joined a small group of like-minded army friends to plan a revolution. With the help of Russian agents, Sukhbaatar's group and a similar nationalist group led by Khorloogiin Choibalsan fled to Siberia, where they received military training from the Russians. When Baron Roman von Ungern-Sternberg drove out the Chinese, Sukhbaatar and his followers moved to Troitskosavsk (now Kyakhta) on the Russian border and formed what would soon become the Mongolian People's Revolutionary Party.

In March 1921, Sukhbaatar crossed the border and drove the Chinese out of the town of Amgalanbaatar. He made it a provisional capital and renamed it Altanbulag.

The baron attacked the revolutionary government. Sukhbaatar, Choibalsan, and the Russian army repulsed his attack, captured the capital city of Urga, and proclaimed the independence of Mongolia on July 11, 1921.

Sukhbaatar died mysteriously in 1923 at the age of thirty. He was once buried in a mausoleum in a central square in Ulaanbaatar, but his remains were moved to a cemetery in 2005. A statue of the young nationalist astride a horse still stands in the square in his honor.

FIGHTING FORCES

In the Russian Revolution of October 1917, the Bolshevik Party's forces successfully fought against the White Russian army of the czar. The Bolsheviks, who became the communists, also helped the Mongolian nationalists in their own struggle for independence.

Khorloogiin Choibalsan (*left*) consults with Soviet general Georgy Zhukov in 1939.

In 1931, Japan invaded Manchuria and threatened to overrun Mongolia, but joint Soviet-Mongolian forces met that threat successfully. Subsequently, Russia and China signed an anti-Japanese treaty that also recognized Mongolia's independence.

When Choibalsan died in 1952, Yumjaagiin Tsedenbal became president. During his long tenure (1952—1984), he promoted Russian culture. Everyone had to speak Russian, schools and universities taught in Russian, and people wore Western-style clothing instead of the *del*, the traditional Mongolian dress. Intellectuals were persecuted for expressing independent views. Tsedenbal was ousted in 1984.

THE MOVE TOWARD DEMOCRACY

In the late 1980s, the Soviet Union implemented perestroika and glasnost, surprisingly liberal policies calling for a restructuring of the economy and greater openness in political affairs. Jambyn Batmonkh, who succeeded Tsedenbal, reorganized the government and decentralized the economy. In July 1990, the first free elections were held. Since the move to democracy, the Mongolian parliament has generally been dominated by the former communist party, which in 2010 changed its name back to the Mongolian People's Party (MPP), sometimes as part of a coalition with other parties. A group of opposition parties won control of the government in the 1996 parliamentary election, but they lost power in the next election, in 2000. Those opposition parties solidified into the Democratic Party, which again won control of parliament in 2012, though the MPP returned to power in 2016.

Whereas the MPP has almost always controlled the Mongolian parliament, candidates from the Democratic Party have fared better in presidential elections. For example, Tsakhiagiin Elbegdorj was elected to two terms as president of Mongolia, in 2009 and 2013. In 2017, he was succeeded by Khaltmaa Battulga, also a Democrat.

The transition to democracy and a free-market system has not been without its growing pains. Over the last decade, a number of demonstrations have taken place pushing for legal reform, mostly in the area of land management and ownership. These protests have generally been peaceful and have actually helped enable the privatization of land. Sadly, not all demonstrations have gone so smoothly. In 2008, hundreds of demonstrators took to the streets of Ulaanbaatar and set fire to the MPRP headquarters to protest alleged election fraud by the party. While these claims were largely discounted, the riot resulted in five deaths, hundreds of injuries, and the imposition of a four-day state of emergency.

Tsakhiagiin Elbegdorj served as president of Mongolia from 2009 to 2017.

INTERNET LINKS

https://www.history.com/topics/genghis-khan
This video and text on the History Channel website examines how Genghis Khan and his fierce warriors expanded the Mongol Empire.

https://www.projects-abroad.org/volunteer-projects/culture-and-community/nomad-project/volunteer-mongolia/#start-dates
Projects Abroad organizes the Nomad Culture Volunteer Project in Mongolia.

https://www.youtube.com/watch?v=9_1oi7mUJPI
"Communist Mongolia 1924–1990" is a video that chronicles the country's communist era.

"You've got China on one side of you, and Russia on the other side of you, and there are always a lot of pressures, and here you are in this oasis of democracy fighting for your own identity."
—John Kerry, former US secretary of state

GOVERNMENT

The Plenary Session Hall of the State Great Hural

3

MONGOLIA'S GOVERNMENT HAS been through many transitions and continues to evolve. For much of its premodern history, it was a feudal society. In the twentieth century, it became a socialist state cut off from the rest of the world. For more than sixty-five years, Mongolia operated under the communist influence of the Soviet Union. When the Soviet Union and Eastern European countries began to dismantle their communist rule, and students protested in China, Mongolia also demonstrated for a change in government. As the twenty-first century neared, Mongolia turned toward democracy. It now embraces a democratic system of government and continues to develop its place among the nations of the world.

"Through its impressive democratic achievements and its progress on economic liberalization, Mongolia serves as a significant example of positive reform and transformation for peoples around the world."

—Barack Obama, president of the United States, 2009-2017

CENTRAL GOVERNMENT

Mongolia has a parliamentary government. The State Great Hural (HOO-rahl), or parliament, is the highest legislative body in the land and has seventy-six members. It appoints the prime minister and members of his cabinet, which is the highest executive body of the state and ensures that all policies of the State Great Hural are implemented. It also oversees the activities of smaller local governments. The national government is led by a president, elected by popular vote. Though the president has powers of veto and has other responsibilities, he is primarily a symbolic figure.

The Supreme Court, which includes the chief justice and other judges, is the highest judicial authority in the land. Judges are appointed by the president. A separate Constitutional Court, also called the Tsets, has authority to rule on questions regarding the country's constitution. Its judges are chosen for six-year terms by the State Great Hural, from a group of candidates put forward by the president, the parliament, and the Supreme Court.

The Mongolian legal system is a blend of Russian, Chinese, and Turkish law. Civil law, which is closely modeled on the Russian system, governs relations between people, protecting their rights and the rights of the family. Civil and criminal cases are settled in the people's district courts and provincial courts.

LOCAL GOVERNMENT

In order to govern Mongolia's large area, the country is divided into twenty-two administrative regions: twenty-one *aimags* (or *aymags*, AI-mugs), or provinces, and the municipality of Ulaanbaatar. The largest aimag is the Gobi Desert region of Omnogovi. This area has 63,690 square miles (165,000 sq km) of land, a very rigorous climate, and is the most sparsely populated aimag, with only 57,200 people.

Each aimag is divided into smaller districts, of which there are 331 in Mongolia. The aimags are governed by small legislative councils called *hural*. Deputies, or representatives of the people, are elected to the hural for four-year terms.

THE MONGOLIAN PEOPLE'S REVOLUTIONARY PARTY

The Mongolian People's Revolutionary Party (MPRP) is Mongolia's oldest—and for a very long time the only—political party in the nation. It ruled the country from 1921 until the political reforms of the 1990s, and it has continued to dominate the Mongolian parliament for much of the time since then. Before the revolution of 1921, there were no political parties in Mongolia.

The MPRP was established on March 1, 1921, at a meeting of seventeen Mongolian revolutionaries in the Russian border town of Troitskosavsk (now Kyakhta). Since the move toward greater political freedom and expression began in the 1990s, the MPRP has shed its former Marxist-Leninist communist philosophy. Instead, now it proclaims democratic socialist principles. In 2010, the MPRP changed its name to the Mongolian People's Party (MPP). It lost control of parliament to the Democratic Party (DP) in 2012. In 2016, the MPP regained control in the government.

GOVERNMENT UNREST

Toward the end of the 1980s, the changes in European communist countries began to have similar impacts on Mongolia. Several newly formed opposition parties organized peaceful demonstrations, demanding political and economic reforms. The most prominent of these fledgling parties was the Mongolian Democratic Union, founded in December 1989.

As new opposition groups emerged and public rallies increased, a crisis of confidence occurred within the ruling Mongolian People's Revolutionary Party (MPRP), and the entire communist leadership of Mongolia resigned. The prime minister, Jambyn Batmonkh, was replaced by Punsalmaagiin Ochirbat as head of government in 1990. The ruling party responded to the people's demands, expelling Yumjaagiin Tsedenbal, its general party secretary, and rehabilitating those purged by him in the 1960s. Foreign investments were encouraged through new laws. Previously, the communist government had enforced collective ownership of all livestock—everything was owned by the state, and the number of animals people could own personally was limited. Such limitations were removed, and new opposition parties were legalized.

Mongolians vote in the 2017 presidential election.

In July 1990, the first democratic general election was held. This brought into existence a parliamentary government with a president and, for the first time, representatives from more than one political party in the State Great Hural. Still, the MPRP had held on to its strong control over government. Of the 430 deputies in the State Great Hural, 357 were MPRP candidates. Also elected were candidates from the Mongolian Democratic Party, the Mongolian Revolutionary Youth League, the Mongolian National Progress Party, and the Mongolian Social-Democratic Party, as well as some independent candidates.

A new constitution in 1992 made two important changes: it reduced the number of members of the State Great Hural to seventy-six, all belonging to the sole legislative house, and it changed the name of the country from the Mongolian People's Republic to, simply, Mongolia. The election results that year showed that the MPRP was still popular; it won seventy out of the seventy-six seats.

The 1996 election gave the opposition parties their first victory. The Democratic Alliance, a coalition of several opposition parties, won fifty seats in the State Great Hural. The MPRP took only twenty-five seats, and the United Heritage Party one. Radnaasumbereliin Gonchigdorj, the leader of the Mongolian Social Democratic Party (a member of the Democratic Alliance), became chairman of the State Great Hural. The leader of the Democratic Alliance, Mendsaikhanu Enkhsaikhan, became the prime minister. The president continued to be Punsalmaagiin Ochirbat, who replaced Jambyn Batmonkh in 1990 and had had his position confirmed by the people in direct elections in 1993. By May 1997, however, Ochirbat's popularity had waned. He lost the presidential election that year to Natsagiin Bagabandi, chairman of the MPRP.

On April 23, 1998, Tsakhiagiin Elbegdorj, leader of the Democracy Union coalition, became Mongolia's youngest prime minister. During the 2000 elections,

POLITICAL PARTIES

In the years following the 1992 election, the opposition parties regrouped. Four of them formed the Mongolian National Democratic Party, and another four parties became the Coalition of Four Unions. A United Heritage Party emerged, as well as the Mongolian Democratic Renewal Party. All of them pressured the government for change and improvements in the people's living standards. Demonstrations and hunger strikes were held in Sukhbaatar Square from 1993 to 1995.

the Mongolian first-past-the-post electoral system—the persons with the most votes win—enabled the MPRP to win 95 percent of the seats in parliament with only 52 percent of the popular vote. This new government was led by Prime Minister Nambaryn Enkhbayar. In 2001, the government amended the constitution to limit one of the main presidential powers, that of nominating the prime minister, to his only naming the candidate proposed by the ruling party. The 2004 elections saw a nearly fifty-fifty split between the MPRP and the Democratic Party. The latter formed a new government under Prime Minister Tsakhiagiin Elbegdorj. This government, however, was short-lived. In 2006, the ten MPRP ministers resigned from the government coalition, leading to the dissolution of the government and the formation of a new coalition government under the MPRP led by Prime Minister Miyeegombyn Enkhbold. Meanwhile, Nambaryn Enkhbayar of the MPRP, formerly the prime minister, had been elected president in 2005.

In October 2007, the prime minister was ousted by the MPRP and replaced by its new leader, Sanjaagiin Bayar. The parliamentary elections of 2008 gave the MPRP a significant majority but triggered violent protests outside the MPRP headquarters because of allegations of rigged voting and election fraud. At least five people were killed and hundreds injured before a state of emergency was declared. Nevertheless, Nambaryn Enkhbayar retained his presidency until the May 2009 elections, when Tsakhiagiin Elbegdorj began his term. He was reelected in 2013. Democratic candidate Khaltmaa Battulga began his term in 2017.

Mongolian soldiers salute as the national flag waves in the background.

A NEW CONSTITUTION

The constitution of Mongolia was adopted in 1960. It was changed in 1992 and further revised in 1996 and 2001. In its present form, it has shed much of its former communist ideology and now reflects the move toward democratic reform of the government and an open-market economy.

The constitution proclaims Mongolia to be an independent and sovereign republic. It upholds the ideals of democracy, justice, freedom, equality, national unity, and respect for the law. Total power is vested in the people and is exercised through their direct participation in state affairs and through elected representatives.

The state recognizes all forms of public and private property, including private ownership of land, but reserves the right to confiscate private land if it has been used for a purpose contrary to the national interest.

Basic human rights and freedoms are guaranteed, including social assistance entitlements in old age, disability, childbirth, and child care. All citizens have the right to free medical care and free basic education.

THE MILITARY

The Mongolian army was at its most formidable in the thirteenth to the sixteenth centuries, at the height of the great Mongol Empire. The modern Mongolian army traces its beginnings to March 1921 when the rebel forces under Damdiny Sukhbaatar and Khorloogiin Choibalsan defeated both Chinese and White Russian army forces to liberate Mongolia from foreign invaders. In 1939, Mongolian forces helped Soviet forces repel a Japanese invasion from Manchuria. Mongolia also gave support to Soviet forces during World War II.

Today, the armed forces are made up of troops for general defense, air defense, construction, and civil defense. All Mongolian males above the age of eighteen are obliged by law to complete one year of active military service. Those who have fulfilled their service are enrolled in the reserves. The Mongolian

DIPLOMATIC RECOGNITION FOR MONGOLIA

After Mongolia declared independence in 1921, the first noncommunist country to give it recognition was India, in 1955. Mongolia became a member of the United Nations in 1961 and was given diplomatic recognition by the United Kingdom and other Western European countries in 1963. The United States recognized Mongolia in 1987.

army has been involved in UN peacekeeping operations in Sierra Leone and Kosovo, and it has also assisted the United States with troop detachments in both Iraq and Afghanistan.

Mongolia has been working to modernize its military strategies and technologies. It is also working on forming a program of military cooperation with neighboring Russia beginning in 2019.

"I do believe that together we shall build a country which has rapid economic growth, high global reputation, developed domestic industry, and creative citizens."
—Khaltmaa Battulga, president of Mongolia

INTERNATIONAL DIPLOMACY

In the 1990s, despite reforms toward democratic freedoms and a market economy, bonds with the Russian Federation (Russia) and the other newly independent countries from the former Soviet Union continued to be strong. Ties with China improved as well, although historically they have not been smooth. Mongolia maintains good relations with numerous other nations, including the United States, Canada, South Korea, and Japan.

INTERNET LINKS

https://www.indexmundi.com/mongolia/government_profile.html
This website offers a detailed profile of Mongolia's government.

https://www.state.gov/r/pa/ei/bgn/2779.htm
US relations with Mongolia are explained on the website of the US Department of State.

ECONOMY

This store owner illustrates the growing opportunities for entrepreneurs in Mongolia.

4

THE DEVELOPMENT OF MONGOLIA'S economy is marked by three distinct periods. Before the revolution, Mongolia had a traditional economy. A socialist economy was in place after 1921 where the government set production quotas for farms and factories. In the late 1980s, Mongolia began transitioning toward an open-market economy. Mongolia has sought to revive the national economy by increasing the proportion of private ownership and drawing in foreign investment by offering favorable conditions. Enterprise by individuals is encouraged. The urban entrepreneurs and the traditional nomadic sheep and cattle herders are equally important to developing the country's economy.

"Over the past twenty-five years, Mongolia has transformed into a vibrant democracy, with three times the level of GDP per capita and increasing school enrollments, and dramatic declines in maternal and child mortality."

—The World Bank

THREE ECONOMIC REGIONS

In the late 1980s, Mongolia was divided into three economic regions. Today, the central region is the most productive. It covers the Selenge, Bulgan, Khovsgol, Tov, Arkhangai, Ovorkhangai, Bayankhongor, Dundgovi, Omnogovi, and Dornogovi aimags. About 70 percent of the population lives in this region, which includes the major industrial centers of Ulaanbaatar, Darkhan, and Erdenet. It has the richest mineral deposits, the best agricultural land, and the most developed network of power supply, transportation, and communications. It is responsible for about 80 percent of the national industrial output and more than 60 percent of the national agricultural yield.

The eastern economic region consists of the Sukhbaatar, Dornod, and Khentii aimags. It occupies one-quarter of the country, and about one-tenth of the people live there. Most of the land is steppeland, which is fertile pastures. The area is rich in mining, mainly of tungsten, fluorspar, and brown coal.

The western economic region includes the Bayan-Olgi, Uvs, Khovd, Zavkhan, and Govi-Altai aimags. It is somewhat more populated than the eastern region—more than 21 percent of the population lives there—but it contributes less than the other regions to the national industrial output. Nevertheless, the western region is believed to be economically promising, especially in mineral resources, which remain to be developed. Animal herding by-products, timber and other building materials, and minerals make up the region's share of the national commerce.

The industrial city of Darkhan

A CHANGING ECONOMY

Traditionally, Mongolia's subsistence economy (providing just enough for a family's needs) was based on nomadic animal husbandry. Most of the population were herders who owned livestock or tended the herds belonging to the rich or the monasteries. They produced necessities from the animals, kept what they needed, and gave the rest as rent. There was hardly any farming or industry. Trade and businesses were run mostly by the Chinese.

After the revolution in 1921, the communist government began to grow crops and launch industries based on the processing of animal products. Mining, forestry, and consumer goods industries, as well as railway and industrial complexes, were developed. The government controlled all trade, finance, transportation, and communications. Collectivization was introduced, livestock taken over from private owners, and state farms established. All production targets were set by the state in five-year plans.

In the late 1980s, however, it dawned on the government that there was overcentralization and that production goals were being met regardless of the many costs. So, the government introduced democratic reforms. Since its privatization policy was implemented, thousands of private businesses have started up, aided by a significant increase in foreign investment. These businesses have boosted the sometimes struggling economy and provided more jobs in a nation where unemployment is about 8 percent. Mongolia's government also maintains state-owned enterprises, especially in the financial and telecommunications sectors.

LIVESTOCK AND CROPS

Yaks graze on the Mongolian steppes.

Raising livestock is still the principal economic activity in Mongolia. The main food product of Mongols is meat. Since collectivization was reversed, herders are allowed to own more animals. Limits on private ownership have been removed. By 1999, more than 96 percent of all livestock was privately owned.

There are more than nineteen million sheep, over 50 percent of all livestock. Wool is produced from sheep and camels. Cattle, horses, goats, and camels provide meat, skins, and milk. Mongolia has industrial cattle farms and mechanized dairies. About 2 million gallons or more (some 7.6 million liters) of *airag* (AI-rug), an alcoholic drink made from mare's milk, are consumed annually.

Farming in Mongolia is very limited and difficult due to the harsh climate. The main crops are grains, mainly wheat. Barley, oats, and millet are grown mostly as fodder for the livestock. Potatoes, cabbages, carrots, turnips, onions, garlic, cucumbers, tomatoes, and lettuce are the main vegetables grown. All produce is consumed domestically.

A truck dumps coal at Mongolia's largest state-owned coal operation in Omnogovi Province.

HARVESTING TIMBER AND FISH

Mongolia's forests yield timber for construction and for fuel. The timber harvest has increased significantly since the mid-1990s, and deforestation at a rate of about 8 percent is beginning to affect both the forestry economy and the environment. Indigenous forest and steppe animals, such as marmots (a member of the squirrel family), squirrels, foxes, wolves, and deer, are hunted for their fur, meat, and other products. Animal hides are exported.

A very small fishing industry produces canned fish that is exported to several markets.

HARVESTING COAL AND MINERALS

Until the 1920s, mining was limited to coal. The Nalaih mine near Ulaanbaatar was the country's oldest coal mine. Mongolia is rich not only in coal but also in copper, fluorspar, gold, iron ore, lead, tin, tungsten, and uranium. In the 1970s, valuable deposits of coal, copper, molybdenum, tin, tungsten, fluorspar, and gold were discovered, transferring the country's economic base from agriculture and herding to mining. While there are significant mining reserves still to be exploited, Mongolia is a leading world producer and exporter of copper, molybdenum, and fluorspar. Mining is an important economic sector, accounting for more than 80 percent of the country's exports.

"Mongolia's growth prospects remain solid for 2018 and 2019. Sustained investment into the mining sector will form a basis for continued growth." —Yolanda Fernandez Lommen, Asian Development Bank country director for Mongolia

FUEL AND ELECTRICITY

Most of the country's coal is used to fuel power stations. Mongolia produces more than 44 million tons (40 million metric tons) of coal a year, a small slice of the country's reserve of at least 100 billion tons (91 billion metric tons).

Power stations are very visible in Ulaanbaatar and other towns. Most aimag centers have steam-driven thermal power plants or diesel generators. In the rural areas, people still gather wood and dry animal dung to use as fuel,

A coal power plant dominates the landscape in Mongolia's capital city of Ulaanbaatar.

often the household chore of children. Portable solar panels are gaining favor among nomadic families to charge their cell phones and power their other electronics, from satellite dishes to televisions.

Some coal is exported to Russia by rail in exchange for electricity. Mongolia imports 90 percent of petroleum products from Russia, making it vulnerable to increases in price that can impact the economy. Mongolia is exploring alternative sources of fuel; it is prospecting for oil and gas, for example, and is developing wind and solar power.

MANUFACTURING

Factories in Ulaanbaatar and Erdenet turn out carpets, knitwear, and products of cashmere wool (the cashmere goat's fine, soft undercoat), camel hair, and felt. Mongolia is the world's second-largest producer of cashmere. The food industry has meat-packing plants, dairies, and flour mills, and produces canned meat, sausages, butter, and other commodities. There are also woodworking, paper, furniture, and construction enterprises that depend on the forestry industry.

This construction site is in Ulaanbaatar.

BUILDING AND PLANTS

The construction industry has been important in modernizing Mongolia. China provided the labor, materials, and expertise to help build brick and glass works, lumber mills, housing developments, and other projects. By the early 1990s, Mongolia had almost one hundred national construction companies in operation.

Today there are more than eight hundred construction companies. There are brick, cement, and reinforced concrete plants, and timber mills in Ulaanbaatar, Darkhan, and other towns. Housing construction continues to keep pace with the increasing population, the majority of which now lives in urban areas. Commercial and residential construction is the third-largest industry, after mining and agriculture.

MODES OF TRANSPORT

Carts—drawn by horse, camel, or yak—have given way to modern road and rail transportation. Construction of the first hard-surface roads began in the late 1920s. In 1925, Mongolia established a state transportation committee with twelve trucks. Mongolia has about 30,600 miles (49,250 km) of roads, but only about 3,000 miles (4,800 km), or about 10 percent, are paved. It is expected that more than 1,200 miles (2,000 km) of new roads will be paved to connect province centers to the capital city of Ulaanbaatar.

Chinggis Khaan International Airport is on the southwestern outskirts of Ulaanbaatar.

THE CONNECTED NOMAD

Many Mongolians still cling to their time-honored way of life herding animals and living in a ger. Yet these traditionalists have kept up with some modern technologies. It is not unusual to see occupants in a ger using their cell phones. When reception is spotty in open areas of the land, nomads will go to the nearest mountaintop or village to use their phones. (In places lacking cell reception, walkie talkies keep people connected.) Nomadic Mongolians use their phones to keep in touch, especially with their children who board at school in towns. They also order supplies and set prices for the meat they sell, and like most everyone who owns a cell phone, they have loaded music and games on it for entertainment. Today's nomad can ride his horse while talking on his cell phone, much like his warrior ancestor who rode a horse while shooting an arrow.

Much of the development of modern transportation was done with Soviet aid, especially roads and bridges. Railroad construction began only in the late 1930s. The Trans-Mongolian Railway links Ulaanbaatar with Moscow in the north and Beijing in the southeast. Almost all of Mongolia's imports and exports are moved by rail.

Water transportation is minimal as Mongolia is landlocked. It has some 360 miles (580 km) of navigable waterways, mainly on Lake Khovsgol and the Selenge River, used for carrying goods to and from Russia.

Air transportation is important because Mongolia's small population is spread over a very large area. Mongolian Airlines, or MIAT, the international carrier, and two other registered carriers, run regular air service to most parts of the country carrying passengers, freight, and mail. Chinggis Khaan International Airport, also known as Ulaanbaatar Airport, is near the capital city. There are also forty-four regional or domestic airports and one heliport spread throughout the country. Mongolia has international air links to several major cities, including Beijing, Berlin, Hong Kong, Moscow, and Seoul.

INFORMATION TECHNOLOGY

In 1921 the new revolutionary government nationalized the postal and telecommunication services that had been Russian-, Chinese-, and Danish-owned, and established a Mongolian postal and telegraph department. Soviet aid helped Mongolia develop its communication networks.

Since then, the communication infrastructure in Mongolia has grown remarkably. The country now counts about 675,000 internet users and several internet and satellite dish providers. Two-thirds of Mongolia's population has television, watching 131 broadcast stations. There are 69 radio stations, more than 200,000 main telephone lines in use, and over 3.3 million cellular phone subscriptions.

This ger on the Mongolian steppes includes a satellite dish.

THE MESSENGER SYSTEM

In the thirteenth century Mongolia had a sophisticated communications system of horse relay. All herders had to contribute horses to this system. Horse relay stations, or ortoo *(OOR-taw), were maintained at intervals of 20 to 30 miles (32 to 48 km) along the main routes crossing the Mongol Empire. A court messenger could arrive at any station and be assured of being fed and rested as well as receiving a fresh mount for the rest of his journey.*

The ortoo system was like the Pony Express that linked the western United States with the developed eastern states from 1860 to 1861, although the Pony Express was mainly a mail service, with stations 25 to 75 miles (40 to 120 km) apart. Unlike the Pony Express riders, who handed their saddlebags to another rider at the next relay station, the Mongolian couriers rode the full distance themselves. They often covered 50 to 70 miles (80 to 113 km) a day and stopped only briefly, if at all, for food and rest. They would strap themselves up tightly with leather belts to keep from falling off their horses if they dozed in the saddle.

The ortoo system helped to build and administer the Mongol Empire by providing quick and efficient communication between the khan and his far-ranging army. It remained in operation until the early twentieth century. In 1913, there were still 150 stations on the main roads that passed through the capital and crossed the country from north to south and from east to west in an effective web.

FINANCIAL INSTITUTIONS

Until 1924, Mongolia did not have any banks of its own—or a currency, either. There was an active barter trade, using livestock, tea, and salt. Within the country, Russian and Chinese currencies were used, while foreign trade was in US dollars and the British pound. Most of the banks that existed at the time were owned by Chinese business interests.

The revolutionary government reformed the system and established the Mongolbank (now known as the Bank of Mongolia) in 1924. A year later, the government introduced the tugrik (also called the togrog) as the national currency. All debts to moneylenders and foreign merchants were canceled, and private lending was outlawed. All state enterprises had to deposit their money

INTERNATIONAL MEMBERSHIPS

Mongolia is a member of several international organizations. It joined the Group of 77 in 1989; the International Monetary Fund, World Bank, and Asian Development Bank in 1991; and the World Trade Organization in 1997. Mongolia is also a member of the World Health Organization.

These Mongolian banknotes feature the revolutionary leader Damdiny Sukhbaatar.

with the state bank, which controlled all financial transactions in the country. Now a western-style banking system is in place, organized into two tiers. The Bank of Mongolia works as the central financial institution in the country, determining monetary policy. Commercial and private financial services are provided by smaller commercial banks.

IMPORTS AND EXPORTS

Before the 1990s, Mongolia's main trading partners were the Soviet Union and Eastern European countries. Trade with other communist countries increased after Mongolia joined the Council for Mutual Economic Assistance (COMECON) in 1962.

Until the 1980s, Mongolia continued to import more than it exported, and the Soviet Union was its major trading partner. Today, Mongolia imports most of its goods from China, Russia, South Korea, and Japan, totaling $4.196 billion. The main imports are machinery and equipment, fuel, cars, food products, industrial consumer goods, chemicals, and building materials. The main export partners are China and the United Kingdom. Mongolia exports mainly mineral products, such as copper, and textiles, such as cashmere and wool, totaling $5.676 billion dollars.

Workers produce cashmere and camel hair sweaters at the Gobi Cashmere Company in Ulaanbaatar.

LABOR FORCE

With economic development, the labor force has grown dramatically—from 1960 to 1983 the number of workers doubled. It now numbers at 1.24 million people, of whom almost half are employed in material production. Most of them have had eight to nine years of schooling. Mongolians generally work an eight-hour day and enjoy fifteen days of paid vacation a year.

Half of Mongolia's workforce, 50.5 percent, is in the service sector. About 31 percent is in agriculture, and 18.5 percent is in the industrial sector. Closure of state enterprises caused a large increase in unemployment in the cities, which peaked in 2003 at about 20 to 25 percent but has since recovered astonishingly to a rate of 8 percent. Despite this improvement, 21.6 percent of the population lives below the poverty line.

Tourists can stay at ger camps to experience nomadic life.

TRAVEL TO MONGOLIA

Tourism is a major industry in Mongolia, making up 9 percent of the annual gross domestic product (GDP). Visitors to Mongolia now number some half a million. The last decade has seen an explosion in the number of tour agencies and hotels, from cheap dormitory-style accommodations to fancy four-star hotels such as Hotel Ulaanbaatar and the Chinggis Khaan Hotel.

The mountains attract climbers, and tourists come to enjoy other outdoor activities, including skiing and ice-skating, camping, hiking, fishing, riding, and kayaking. There are tourist gers, too, so the visitor can get a taste of living Mongolian style.

Popular tourist destinations include the capital city of Ulaanbaatar; the Gorkhi-Terelj National Park northeast of the capital; the Gobi Gurvansaikhan National Park; and the Altai Tavan Bogd National Park, home to the traditional eagle hunters.

INVESTING IN BUSINESS

The Mongolian Stock Exchange (MSE) was created in 1991 as part of the country's program to privatize state-owned companies and develop a capital market. From 1992 to 1995, there was free distribution of vouchers to all Mongolian citizens for buying shares in companies on the state exchange. Then, starting in August 1995, the MSE began functioning as a regular stock exchange, with a listing of 470 companies. The Mongolian Securities Commission, created in 1995, is charged with regulating and controlling activities in the securities market. The coal trade has helped bump up Mongolia's stock index with an average 5.3 percent growth in 2017.

SUPPLY AND DEMAND

The change to a market economy caused an economic crisis in the early 1990s with the collapse of trade and foreign aid ties with the former Soviet

Union. Industrial production dropped because of fuel shortages and distribution problems, and basic foodstuffs had to be rationed. Inflation was 325 percent in 1992. After the opposition came to power in 1996, wide-ranging economic reforms were implemented. Government spending was cut, insolvent banks were closed, utility prices were raised, and foreign investment was welcomed. Inflation dropped to 35 percent, and a four-year economic program was announced that allowed more private ownership of state property.

The Mongolian Stock Exchange is based in Ulaanbaatar.

Mongolia's economy saw rapid growth between 2004 and 2008, spurred mainly by high copper prices and increased gold production. This, in turn, caused inflation to skyrocket to over 40 percent. The weakening global economy in 2008 started to lower the inflation rate significantly and took a toll on Mongolia's exports. Economic recovery is expected to continue in Mongolia through 2019, with a projected inflation rate of 7 percent. Investments in mining will continue to build the economy, but issues with transportation in this landlocked nation could lower coal exports from matching those of previous years.

INTERNET LINKS

https://www.heritage.org/index/country/mongolia

The Index of Economic Freedom details Mongolia's economic standing in the world.

http://www.unv.org/our-stories/un-volunteers-fao-create-agricultural-employment-opportunities-mongolia

This website discusses how United Nations volunteers with the Food and Agriculture Organization help create agricultural jobs for people in rural areas.

https://www.wttc.org/-/media/files/reports/economic-impact-research/countries-2017/mongolia2017.pdf

The economic impact of travel and tourism in Mongolia is assessed by the World Travel and Tourism Council.

ENVIRONMENT

Smog rises above the capital city of Ulaanbaatar.

5

MONGOLIA HAS A LONG TRADITION of a pastoral and nomadic people. In recent decades, Mongolians have found that their rural environs have suffered as Mongolia takes its place among developing countries in the twenty-first century. As more Mongolians quickly transition from a traditional way of life to a more modern one, the environment has been forgotten in the process. Deforestation, desertification, and air and water pollution are some of the serious environmental problems facing Mongolia today. However, Mongolia is learning from the environmental mistakes made and rectifying them. Implementing laws and better controls has helped to correct some of the adverse effects of progress on the environment.

"Air pollution has become a child health crisis in Ulaanbaatar, putting every child and pregnancy at risk."

—Alex Heikens, UNICEF Mongolian representative

The landscape of Mongolia shows the effects of drought.

A DELICATE ECOSYSTEM

Mongolia is in the center of the Asian continent, and much of its land is in high altitude. Its climate is harsh, cold, and dry for much of the year. The summer season is short, making the growing of crops always difficult. Mongolia gets very little rain. Most of the rain falls in the northern parts of the country during a three-month period in the summer. The average in the north is 12 inches (300 millimeters) per year. In the mostly desert south of Mongolia, rain amounts are below 8 inches (200 mm) per year. These amounts are far less than the rain that falls on the state of California (22.2 inches, or 564 mm) and even less than what Arizona receives (13.6 inches or 345 mm).

The country endures regular droughts every two or three years. Its southern regions are very dry and are covered by semidesert or desert land. Its latitude, the generally high altitude of the land, and its location in the middle of the continent result in extreme temperatures; winter temperatures are low and freezing over much of the country. As a result, the soil is thin and the ecosystem is fragile and easily disturbed.

A PUSH TO ADVANCEMENT

In the past, Mongolians lived in accordance with what the land and climate would allow. Their traditional lifestyle has been shaped by the nature of their country. In the 1950s, there began a move to change the nomadic, pastoral, and somewhat agricultural economy to one that was to be more industrial. In order to make Mongolia more developed and progressive, the government pushed for intensive agriculture and industrialization by exploiting the rich mineral resources, speeding up urbanization, and encouraging rapid economic development. Thus, little thought was given to planning, managing the fragile environment, or ensuring the renewability of resources.

Statistically speaking, 73 percent of the land (280 million acres, or 113 million hectares) is used for agriculture and animal husbandry, giving the misleading impression that much of the country is highly productive. However, less than 1 percent of the agricultural land is used for growing crops, while the rest is used as permanent pastureland. Much of the small amount of farmland is found in the northern aimags of Tov and Selenge, where nearly 60 percent of the country's agriculture takes place.

The Gobi Desert in the south is barren and inhospitable to human economic activity. Furthermore, it is expanding over the grasslands by nearly 2,250 square miles (5,827 sq km) each year.

OVERTAXING THE LAND

Bad farming practices and overgrazing of the steppes have caused the rapid deterioration of the land. Between 1960 and 1989, the area that was taken under cultivation increased greatly, with wheat being the main crop. There was intensive tilling of the raw land with little or no attention given to protecting

Animals overgrazing on grasslands has led to desertification.

the soil. This caused erosion and deterioration of the soil quality, resulting in reduced fertility of the small amount of arable land that Mongolia has and leading to the abandonment of much of the vast wheat fields.

As with farming, poor animal husbandry practices contributed to the desertification of the land. Herders became increasingly more settled and tended to roam less. This resulted in pastures being overgrazed, especially since the herds of animals had grown larger. Since 1990, the number of cattle near Ulaanbaatar has doubled, thanks in part to the privatization of the herds and an increase in the human population. Pasturelands, especially around the capital, became seriously overgrazed. The lack of good pasture led to poorer quality of animals and related products. Like the bad farming practices, overgrazing caused soil erosion and the thinning of the steppe grasses.

A third factor in the process of desertification was deforestation. The move to a free market economy in the 1990s was hard on Mongolia's forests. Rapid privatization of land ownership, a lack of effective governmental oversight, and an increase in the demand for timber (for fuel and for the building and woodworking industries) caused an unsustainable jump in the size of timber harvests. Overall, the area of Mongolia's forests has been reduced by 12 percent since 1990. As the trees are cut down or are lost to forest fires and insect damage, the resulting deforestation contributes to more soil erosion. Trees, plants, and grasses together provide protection for the soil from the sun and the wind. They stabilize the soil with their roots, shade the earth, prevent moisture from being sucked up by the intense heat of the sun, and break the force of the wind that stirs up dust storms.

Climate change, which is affecting the whole planet, is another contributing factor to desertification. In Mongolia, this global phenomenon has caused a gradual reduction in the country's annual rainfall, further accelerating soil erosion. Deforestation, overgrazing, and agricultural use of previously unfarmed land continue to severely affect the country's environment.

A POLLUTED ENVIRONMENT

Mongolia's environmental problems do not stop at desertification and deforestation. The country's air and water quality have also suffered from the impact of increased economic activity and a fast-growing population. In the 1990s, Mongolia's population growth rate was one of the highest in Asia, at 2.7 percent per year, but this has decreased, with the population growth rate for 2017 at 1.18 percent. More than half of Mongolia's population—which not long ago was a very rural people—now lives in urban centers. While the majority of people in towns and cities have access to clean drinking water, people living in rural areas are not as fortunate. In 2015, 66 percent of the urban population and 59 percent of the rural population had access to clean drinking water. Even today, many rural families have to draw water in buckets from village wells and carry it back to their homes. Housing, transportation, solid and liquid waste-management facilities, and other infrastructure developments have not kept pace with the growing demands of a larger population and economic development. One-third of the total population of Mongolia still lack clean drinking water.

Polluted waters are a consequence of the mining industry's growth.

Water quality is a constant problem, due in large part to the relative lack of proper sewage systems and water-treatment facilities. Poor housing in urban areas, rapid industrialization, and economic development without adequate controls have resulted in the contamination of the air, water, soil, and groundwater. The rapid rise in the demand for water has caused an ominous drop in lake and river water and in groundwater levels.

The single biggest source of water pollution in Mongolia comes from irresponsible mining and petroleum extraction practices. Until very recently, these activities were done with little government regulation. If there were regulatory laws, they were very poorly enforced. Companies extracting oil did not pay much attention to the risk of oil leaching into the ground. Many mines dumped their wastes wherever it was easiest and cheapest, even if it was close to freshwater sources that could become contaminated. Outdated

THE BLUE PEARL OF MONGOLIA

Lake Khovsgol in northern Mongolia contains around 70 percent of the nation's total reservoir of freshwater. The 85-mile- (137 km) long crystal-clear mountain lake supports a large and diverse ecosystem that is mainly undisturbed by humans, thanks to its remote location and harsh winter climate.

mining techniques and equipment involved the heavy use of chemicals such as mercury and cyanide. This meant that there was a great risk that these toxic chemicals and the oil might leach into the groundwater supply.

The leather industry is another culprit for water pollution. Leather, mostly produced near the capital, Ulaanbaatar, requires large quantities of chemicals such as lime, ammonium chloride, sodium sulfide, and various sulfates in the tanning process. The highly alkaline combination of lime and sodium sulfide is dangerous to workers who are preparing the leather and is often simply washed down the drain or dumped on the ground. This tanning waste, which makes up nearly half of the total waste from leather processing, gradually finds its way into the ground, contaminating enormous quantities of groundwater.

The problem with air quality is concentrated mainly in the urban areas. The air in towns and cities is polluted largely by the coal and wood fuel used by power plants, industries, and cooking and heating stoves of individual dwellings, and by the dirty engine emissions of vehicles. Mongolia experiences annual periods of very low wind and wide temperature fluctuations from late fall to early spring. During these periods, the high levels of particulates in the air frequently reach proportions that are hazardous to health and put young children and the elderly at risk for lethal respiratory illnesses.

A large swath of land shows the effects of soil erosion.

AN ENVIRONMENTAL PLAN

In 1993, Mongolia initiated a National Environmental Action Plan outlining steps to ensure that environmental concerns would be linked to the country's overall economic and social development. Architects of the plan looked at the environmental situation and worked out how Mongolia could manage its natural resources, deal with its pollution and environmental hazards, and conserve its natural heritage. Mongolia's Ministry for Nature and Environment got much-needed help from international environmental specialists to assess and monitor the action plan.

Mongolia is slowly starting to see improvements being made across the country. Land regulations were introduced in 1995 and 2000. New land-management techniques have been introduced with the help of the World Bank and associated international agencies such as the International Development Association. For instance, the planting of trees around agricultural lands has been encouraged to reduce soil erosion caused by wind. With a growing national awareness of Mongolia's environmental problems, the situation is improving. The government recognizes that there are many unique features of the country that need to be safeguarded. Forest and wildlife preserves have thus been created, and endangered animal species are now protected by law and public education.

In the twenty-first century, environmental associations such as the UN-supported Partnership for Action on Green Economy will help Mongolia pace its economic development at a speed commensurate with what the land can sustain.

CONSERVING LAND, THREATENING A CUTURE

In northern Mongolia, along the Russian border, is a region called the snow forest, or taiga. The remote area has been home to the Dukha ethnic minority group for thousands of years. These reindeer herders live close to the land and their animals and rely on them for everything they may need, from food to tools. Now, the Dukha's old way of life is being threatened by new land conservation programs. Mongolia has designated the taiga a protected area in order to preserve its biodiversity and mineral and animal resources. Rangers patrol the forest where the Dukha are now forbidden to hunt or take their reindeer to graze on protected pastures.

PROTECTING THE LAND AND ANIMALS

Mongolia has one of the most varied combinations of climatic zones of any Asian nation. These zones include flood plains, forests, tundra, taiga, salty marshes, freshwater sources, steppes, semidesert, and the fifth-largest desert area in the world. This diversity has made Mongolia home to numerous animal species, including 139 types of mammals, 450 varieties of birds, 76 kinds of fish, 22 reptile species, and 6 different amphibians.

The wild fauna have to compete with domesticated herds for pasture and water. Livestock herds in Mongolia have significantly increased in size to number more than sixty million and threaten to overwhelm the capabilities of the land to support them. These herds of goats, sheep, and cattle eat up ever-widening swaths of grassland, leaving slim pickings for the much smaller, more dispersed groups of wild ungulates such as deer.

This sweeping view of Gorkhi-Terelj National Park is from the monastery within the park.

The growing human population of Mongolia is also creating new communities that impact the land. There are many more people traveling through areas once roamed only by small groups of nomads. The frequent droughts and the long dry season, combined with the carelessness of the people, have caused forest and grass fires to increase, harming the habitat of the Mongolian gazelles, roe deer, red deer, and musk deer. Many of these animal species are in danger of becoming extinct. Rare species, such as the musk deer, are being threatened by a decade-long increase in illegal hunting. Some herdsmen hunt seeking a variety in their diet, but it is mainly poachers who make a quick profit selling rare animal organs and other parts on the black market. These predatory groups are often well organized and heavily armed, posing a problem for the Mongolian border guards and park rangers. Moreover, lack of funds makes it difficult to hire and train enough staff to maintain the parks, fend off poachers, and enforce pollution laws. However, the number of protected areas and nature preserves have increased. Since 1992, areas declared as protected or as national reserves or parklands have more than tripled. In 2012, Mongolia's Department of Protected Areas Management approved a set of standards to develop plans for the management of the nation's protected lands.

The Great Gobi Strictly Protected Area is Mongolia's largest and probably most important preserve. At over 20,500 square miles (53,100 sq km), the

THE LAST WILD HORSE

The Przewalski's horse is named for Russian colonel, explorer, and naturalist Nikolai Przhevalsky, who led an expedition in 1881 to find the last true wild horse in the world. Unlike its "wild" cousins, such as the American mustang, which is actually a domesticated horse gone feral, the Przewalski's horse was believed to have never been domesticated. However, a newer genetic study suggests that the Przewalski's horse is also a feral animal descended from horses that were domesticated 5,500 years ago in Kazakhstan. This short, stocky breed stands at around 13 hands (52 inches, or 1.33 m) and is 20.6 hands (83 inches, or 2.1 m) in length, with a 35-inch (89-centimeter) tail, and has pale brown flanks, a yellowish white belly, and a stiff, dark-brown mane.

By 1969, these horses—also known as the Asian wild horse, the Mongolian wild horse, or the Takhi—had become extinct in the wild. At that time, the only remaining Przewalski's horses left in the world were in zoos in the German city of Munich and the Czech city of Prague. Both populations were based on animals captured in the early 1900s.

Decades after the last Przewalski's horse was spotted in the wild, these wonderful animals are returning. Sixteen horses were reintroduced into Mongolia in 1992, and amazingly the breed appears to be thriving. Though still critically endangered, the population has grown to about four hundred in the wild in Mongolia, with more in reserves and zoos around the world. With careful management and protection, the Przewalski's horse may again become a more common sight on the vast steppes of Mongolia.

Great Gobi area includes both arid and semiarid land, ranging from vast plains and narrow valleys to rugged mountain ranges. The Great Gobi is home to over 410 species of plants, 150 species of birds, 15 different species of reptiles and amphibians, and 49 species of mammals. The dry and rocky area contains some of the rarest species of animals on the planet, including the world's only desert bear, the Gobi bear (*Ursus arctos gobiensis),* the wild Przewalski's horse, and Mongolia's last remaining wild Bactrian camels. The Great Gobi has been nominated for UNESCO World Heritage recognition.

Other notable parks and protected zones include the Gorkhi-Terelj National Park, famed for its rock-climbing areas, the Yestii hot spring, and the Uvs Nuur Strictly Protected Area, which comprises four separate sections: Uvs Nuur, Tiirgen Uul, Tsagaan Shuvuut, and Altal Els. Together, these four areas represent nearly every type of climate in Mongolia, from deserts to snowfields and from forests to marshlands. The park is also home to numerous rare and endangered species such as the snow leopard (*Panthera uncia*).

INTERNET LINKS

http://mongolia.panda.org/en/about_mongolia/wildlife
The World Wildlife Federation (WWF) lists conservation efforts for endangered species in Mongolia.

https://www.nature.org/ourinitiatives/regions/asiaandthepacific/mongolia/index.htm
Land and water conservation in Mongolia is discussed at this website of the Nature Conservancy.

https://www.unicef.org/mongolia/Mongolia_air_pollution_crisis_ENG.pdf
"Mongolia's Air Pollution Crisis: A Call to Action to Protect Children's Health" is a discussion paper issued by the National Center for Public Health and UNICEF.

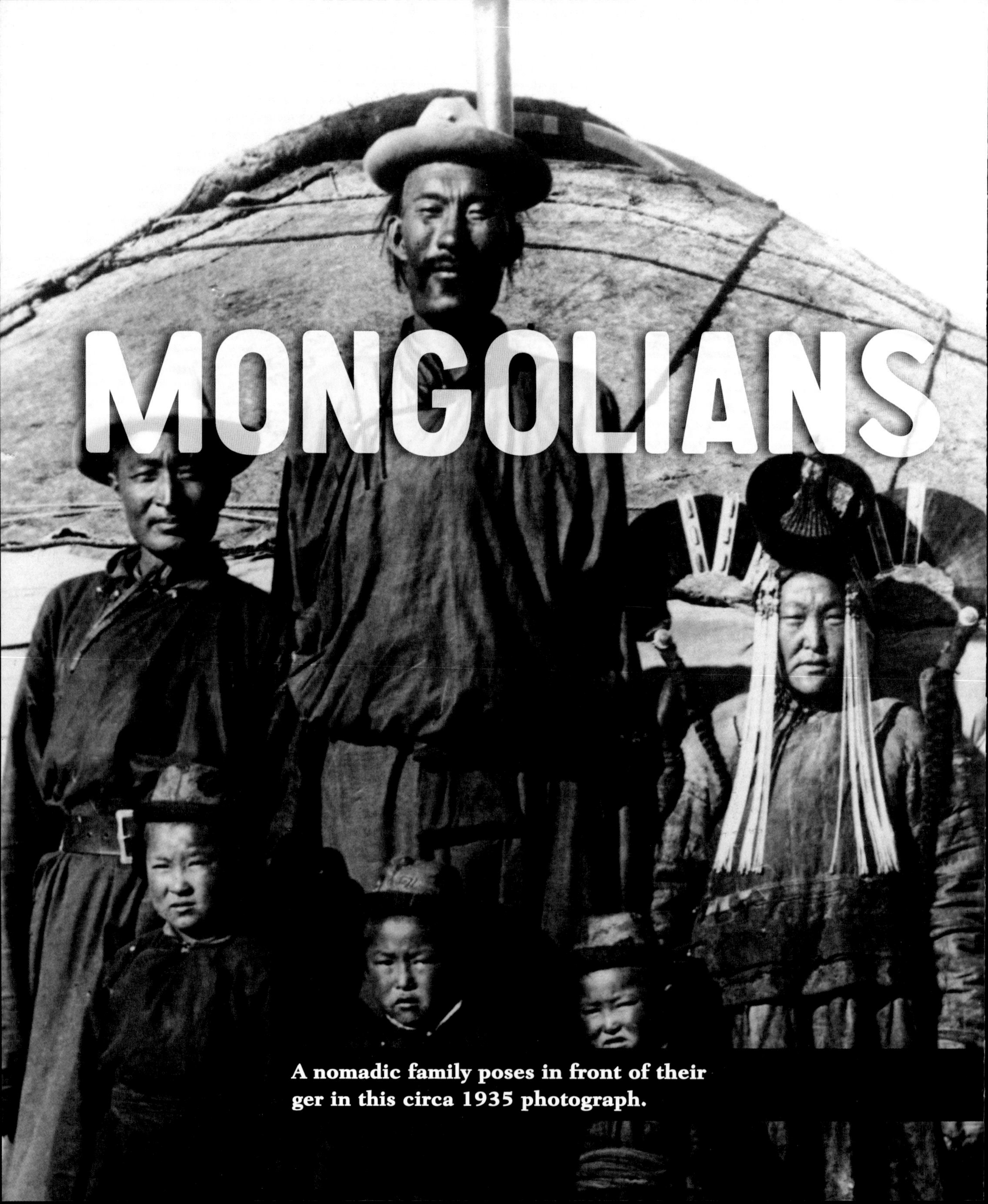

MONGOLIANS

A nomadic family poses in front of their ger in this circa 1935 photograph.

6

MONGOLIANS ARE PERHAPS BEST known for their ancient empire. In the thirteenth century, when the Mongol Empire was at its greatest, its people were known and feared across many lands. In later centuries, Mongolia was closed to the Western world, and its people were largely unknown. Modern Mongolia is open and accessible, and its people are incorporating new ways with old traditions. Mongolia is also one of the more sparsely populated nations in the world, and its population is unevenly distributed across the country. The most densely populated areas are the river valleys of forested mountain slopes and the grasslands. The least populated regions are the desert, semidesert, and mountainous regions.

"Mongolia is a country of rich and ancient heritage, unique culture and astounding beauty. It is a land of free and brave, peace-loving and hard-working people."
—Tsakhiagiin Elbegdorj, president of Mongolia, 2009-2017

POPULATION CHANGES

Mongolia is a fast-growing society. Since the early 1920s, improvements in health care and living standards have made it possible for the population to rapidly increase. Just before the revolution, there were only about half a million people. The population then increased more than sixfold, a growth rate significantly higher than the rest of the world. The growth rate peaked at 2.6 percent in 1992 but has since declined to 1.18 percent. As a result, Mongolia went through a period of having a very young society. In 2008, over one-third of the population was under fifteen years of age, and two-thirds of the population was under the age of thirty. Now the largest segment of the population, more than 45 percent, is between the ages of twenty-five and fifty-four.

As the country continues to modernize and industrialize, the migration of people from rural areas to the cities is increasing. In 2017, 68.4 percent of the Mongolia's total population was concentrated in urban areas.

Family size in Mongolia has seen a drop from an average of 5 people per household to just over 3 in urban areas and just over 3.5 in rural ones. Better health care has increased the life expectancy of the average Mongolian man to 65.7 years and of the average woman to 74.4 years. There used to be more men than women among the population, but now the proportion is almost equal.

THE ETHNICITY OF MONGOLIA

There are two main ethnic groups: the Mongolian group and the Turkic group. The majority of the people fall into the Mongolian group. Of the total population of Mongolia, 81.9 percent are the nomadic Khalkha Mongols who live mainly in the eastern and central part of the country. The word *khalkha* (HAL-ha), meaning "shield," originated around the seventeenth century when the various clans of Mongols of the east formed an alliance in their struggle against the Manchu, or Qing, dynasty of China.

The other peoples in the Mongolian group are the Dorvod, Buryat, Barga, Uzem-chin, Darhad, Zakhchin, Bayad, Myangat, Dariganga, Oold, Torguut, Kharchin, Chahar, and Hotgon. These Mongols live mainly in the west and northwest and along the southeast border with China. The differences among these groups and their dialects are small, so they understand each other easily. Their ethnic clothing varies only slightly from group to group, perhaps simply in the kind of headdress worn or in the shape of the shoes.

A Kazakh boy leads his two horses.

The second ethnic group are the Turkic people. Kazakhs, the largest Turkic group, make up 3.8 percent of the population. They are pastoral people, traditionally Muslim, and they live mainly in the Altai region situated in the extreme western part of the country. They are renowned hunters who pursue their quarry on horseback and use trained golden eagles and greyhounds to attack prey. Many Kazakhs work in the coal mines of north-central Mongolia. Tuvinians, Uriankhai, and Uyghurs are other Turkic peoples.

A small number of Russians and Chinese live permanently in Mongolia. In the early 1920s, many Chinese in Mongolia were merchants, traders, and artisans who worked in the Buddhist monasteries. Many Russians came to Mongolia as advisers and skilled workers during the communist period, married Mongol women, had children, and became assimilated into the local population.

AN ANCIENT SOCIAL SYSTEM

Before the 1921 revolution, Mongolian culture was a fixed feudal society with no social mobility. At the top were the lords claiming descent from Genghis Khan. The commoners worked for the feudal lords, herding their livestock and doing military service when called to it.

There was very little formal education, and it was difficult to change one's status in society. The only "escape" route was through the Buddhist monasteries. Young boys and men might offer their service to the monasteries

A group of women work in the fields.

where, by choosing a monastic career, they could get an education. From the waning of the empire in the sixteenth century to the beginning of the twentieth century, the influence of the Lamaist Buddhist religion resulted in almost half of the male population becoming monks. The lamas, or monks, were a politically and socially powerful class in feudal Mongolian society, but their influence was curbed when the communists came to power in the 1920s.

Most of the population, about 90 percent, were common serfs and lowly monks. The aristocrats, who formed about 8 percent of the population, were the political leaders and administrators.

A REORGANIZED SOCIETY

The structure of Mongolian society underwent major changes after the revolution, as feudalism was seen as contrary to communism. Power and wealth were stripped away from the feudal lords and the powerful monasteries and were redistributed among the people. Mongolian herders, who used to be self-sufficient, were organized into herding collectives or attached to state factories and mines. These herding collectives have now ceased to exist. A monetary system was introduced, and people earned wages for their work. They were supervised by a new class of managers and administrators belonging to the Mongolian People's Revolutionary Party.

Much emphasis was placed on planning projects and meeting goals and targets. Everything was done for the collective good of society. Workers and their units competed to do a job quickly or surpass a production quota. They received benefits such as free medical care, education, and pensions when they retired. Those who excelled at their jobs were honored as "number one" workers. Most working people were party members.

A formal education became important, and most young Mongolians were enrolled in schools where they also learned the new party ideology. They were taught punctuality, rules and standards, and the totally novel need to meet production goals.

The bureaucrats and high-ranking party members were the elite. Next came the professionals—technicians, engineers, doctors, and others. These citizens had access to postsecondary education. Then there were the administrators and workers in the factories and on state farms. Living on the fringes were the traditional nomadic herders whose livelihood depended on the weather and health of their animals, and the performance of their new herding collective.

"Their ancestors lived in the same way for a thousand years, feeling the change of the seasons like moods and moving with them. Their knowledge of this land is ancient, the wind is their breath, the earth is their bed and the dust of the steppe runs in their blood."
—Ian D. Robinson, *Gantsara: Alone Across Mongolia*

TRADITONAL MONGOLIAN CLOTHES

The traditional garment for both Mongolian men and women is a long, flowing robe tied at the waist by a sash. It looks much like a dressing gown that is fastened from the throat and down the right shoulder by small cloth buttons. It has a small stand-up collar. This gown is called the *del*.

Beneath the del, Mongolians wear heavy trousers that are tucked into leather or felt knee-high boots with pointed toes. These boots are worn several sizes too large so that as the weather gets colder, thick socks of wool, felt, or fur can be used to pad the boots, keeping the wearer's feet warm and comfortable. Russian army boots are also very popular.

A modern nomadic family is dressed in colorful traditional clothes.

Both the del, which reaches down to below the knees, and the sash are often very colorful. The del is commonly worn in rural areas. In the winter, it has an inner lining of sheepskin or red fox fur that keeps the wearer warm. The colors and shapes of dels differ according to the different ethnic groups.

In the summer, men sometimes wear a Western-style felt hat or Russian-style cap; in the winter, a warmer fur cap with earflaps is worn to keep the ears warm.

City people, especially office workers, are more often seen in Western-style outfits. The women wear dresses and the men shirts, suits, and shoes. Almost everybody, however, has a special festive del reserved for formal occasions.

The young people in Mongolian towns are like their contemporaries in other cities in the world. Boys love wearing jeans, shirts, and jackets; the

FAMOUS MONGOLIANS

Dashdorjiin Natsagdorj (1906–1937) is considered the father of contemporary Mongolian literature. Most Mongolians know by heart his famous poem "My Motherland," which portrays Mongolia as an old country renewed with a glorious future. The "Four Seasons of the Year" is about building a new Mongolia. The poem "Star" explores the possibility of flights into space. Natsagdorj was also a playwright and the author of Three Tragic Fates, *the first Mongolian opera.*

Balduugiin Sharav (1869–1939), a celebrated painter, spent his childhood in a monastery and later traveled all over Mongolia. The frequent subjects of his paintings were the simple life and traditions of the people. He used traditional techniques. One Day in the Life of Mongolia, *his masterpiece, is full of intricate drawings depicting many aspects of Mongolian life.*

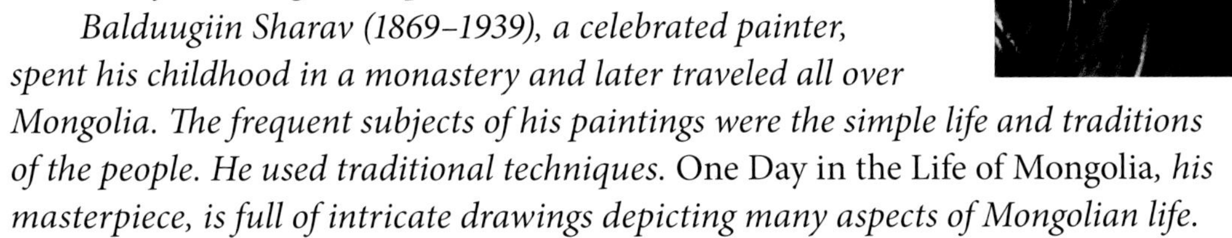

girls wear dresses. Women wear their hair long and often braided or coiled at the back of the head. When a Mongol woman gets married, she is dressed in traditional finery that usually includes an extremely elaborate headdress and heavy jewelry of silver and semiprecious stones. The style of the headdress varies from one ethnic group to another.

INTERNET LINKS

https://www.discovermongolia.mn/mongolian-traditional-clothes
Information and photographs about Mongolia's national dress are available on the website of the tourism company Discover Mongolia.

https://www.metmuseum.org/toah/keywords/mongolia
The Metropolitan Museum of Art has a collection of early Mongolian warrior and horse armor.

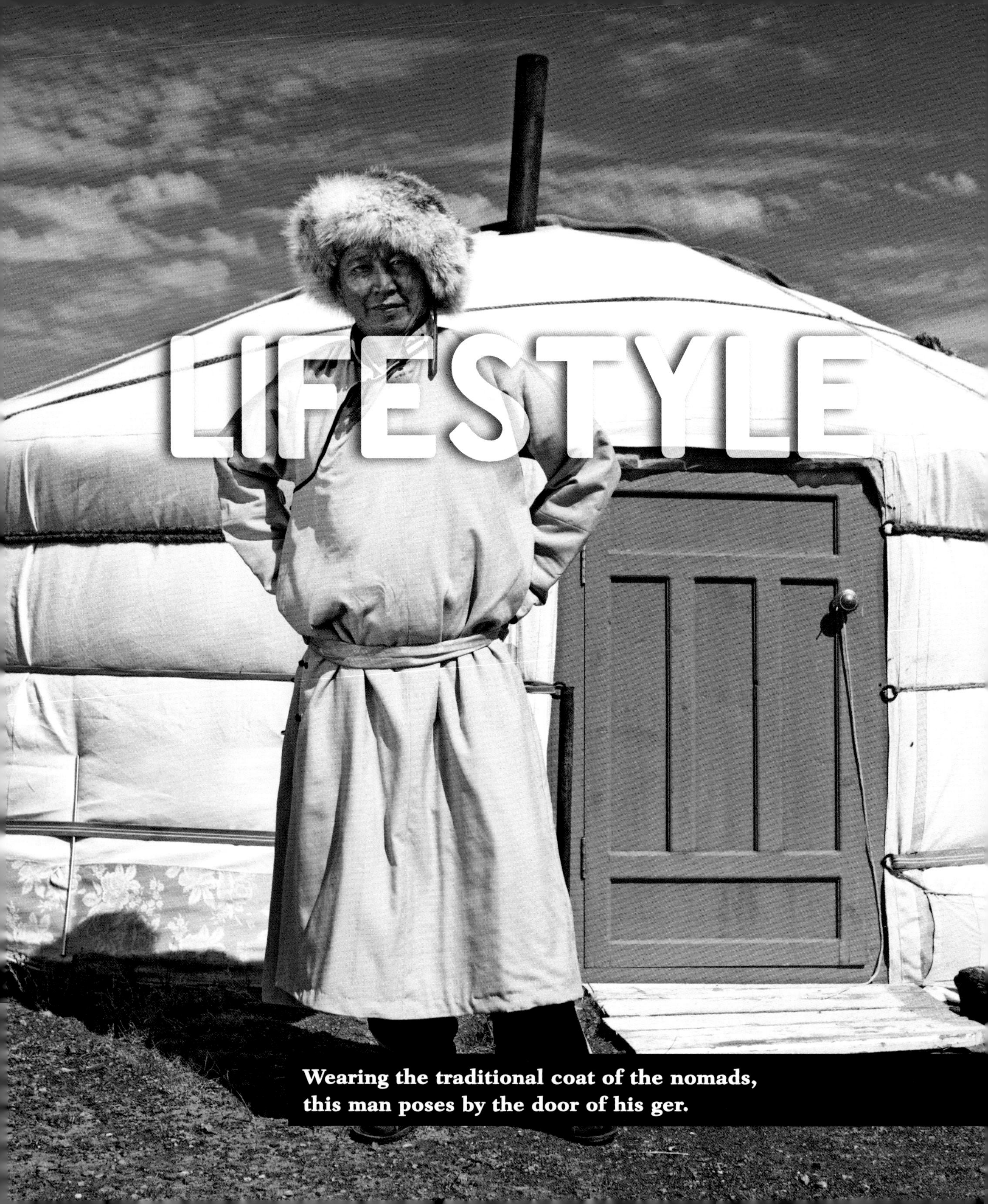

LIFESTYLE

Wearing the traditional coat of the nomads, this man poses by the door of his ger.

7

MODERN MONGOLIA IS A BLEND OF the old and new. Mongolians highly prize and revere the old pastoral ways of life and the open land. They have a close affinity with nature and animals that shapes the lives of many Mongolians. Even city dwellers find a way to connect with the land from time to time. However, while hanging on to old ways, Mongolians have embraced new opportunities. Education offers more options for different kinds of employment. Women, too, have more possibilities for education and are more independent than their traditional ancestors. Modern medicine has found a place in Mongolia while respecting the old traditions of healing.

"I was born in a ger, I grew up in a ger, I got married in a ger. I have never lived in a house. I love my ger."
—Tagtokhbayar Tuvaan

LEGENDS OF THE GER

A legend says that the first Mongol was born after a fair-haired man came through the opening at the top of the ger and impregnated Alangua, the mother of the Mongols. In the nomadic society of the Mongolians, a community is based on helping one another. It is said that the ger door is seldom locked even when the family is out. Any weary traveler can enter to warm himself by the fire, have a rest, and take some food. For the nomads, a visitor is very welcome as days on the steppes can be long and lonely.

A young girl herds sheep on snow-covered grasslands.

AN OLD WAY OF LIFE MADE NEW

Traditional livestock herding has been modernized. Horses are still important but are supplemented with jeeps, trucks, and motorcycles. Herders can get the latest weather reports and storm warnings on radio. At winter camps, portable power generators provide energy.

A herding camp has two to six households, sometimes of related families, managing the livestock together. A family can be part of one camp one year and move on to another the next, although some families remain with one camp for a long time. Herders do not own any grazing ground, but there is an understanding that each camp has the right to use certain areas.

During the summer months, herds are moved over vast areas to places with good grazing land and abundant water. In the wintertime, the camp moves to a site where there is water, dried grass, and shelter from storms. Weaker animals that are not expected to survive the harsh winter are killed in the late fall to reduce the herd size. The meat is dried and stored for the winter when neither sheep nor horses produce milk.

NECESSARY LIVESTOCK

Mongolians have always depended for their well-being on five animals—horses, camels, sheep, cattle or yaks, and goats. These are known as the "five snouts," or the "five muzzles," and they appear in every aspect of Mongolian life, art, and literature. Not every herder has all five, but many have more than one type. The horse is the most important. It is seldom used as a draft animal, but is ridden. It also provides products such as mare's milk to make the alcoholic drink airag, horsehair rope, and horsehide leather. Apart from the meat, milk, and other dairy products, dried dung of the various animals is used as fuel. Leather goods are made from the hides. In the mountains, the yak, a hardy type of ox, is particularly useful. Camels are beasts of burden in the desert and are used for transportation. Sheep's and goat's wool are used for winter clothing and for making the felt that is used to cover the ger. The men and boys look after the horses, while the women tend the other animals.

Goats graze on the Mongolian steppes.

THE NOMAD'S HOUSE

Mongolians traditionally live in a dome-shaped structure called a ger, also called a yurt. Its portability makes it ideal for a nomadic lifestyle. Although apartment buildings are found in cities, most Mongolians in the countryside and small towns still live in gers. Even in Ulaanbaatar, the capital, clusters of gers dot the city's outskirts. City gers often have electricity, while those in rural areas may depend on candles and lamps for lighting. Portable solar panels are becoming more common among rural gers, however.

A large brick or metal stove for heat and cooking stands in the middle, its stovepipe rising through a roof vent. At the sides of the ger, there may be some low, steel-framed beds curtained off. There are large decorated storage chests for clothing and other items, and a few mirrors, photographs, and religious pictures hang on the walls. A low table and some small metal folding chairs occupy the space around the stove. The wooden floor is covered with rugs. The man's working tools, his saddle, and the leather bag containing airag are on his side on the left, under the sky god's protection; the kitchen

"Man's joy is in wide-open and empty spaces."
—Mongolian saying

ERECTING A GER

The wooden floor of the ger is assembled first. Next, the lattice walls are joined end to end to form the lower, circular part of the ger, and the door, which always faces south, is put in place. The walls are made of thin wooden strips fastened in a crisscross lattice, enabling the wall to be opened and shut like an accordion. The size of the ger depends on the number of lattice walls; there may be up to twelve walls in a large structure.

When the circular wall is finished, two wooden posts are set up in the middle of the floor. The small wooden wheel forming the opening in the roof is carefully balanced on them. Long roof poles, painted orange like the sun, are inserted into slots on the wheel so that they radiate from the center like the ribs of a big umbrella. Then, the lower ends of the poles are attached to the lattice walls with leather loops. A layer of canvas is stretched tightly over the roof. Thickly padded felt curtains are hung from the walls for insulation. Then, layer upon layer of felt is spread on the roof. In the winter, more felt layers are piled on. Finally, the whole structure is covered with white canvas to keep out the rain. The hole at the top is covered by a small triangle of canvas, adjusted by cords from the floor. It can be opened to let in light and air and allow smoke to leave, or closed in bad weather. A second, smaller ger may be erected for extra storage space.

The average weight of a ger without furniture is about 550 pounds (250 kilograms). It takes about an hour and a half to erect it. When the family moves, the ger is taken down and placed on a cart pulled by yaks, camels, or horses. Nowadays, it might be loaded onto a pickup truck instead.

Interior view of a ger

and cooking utensils are on the woman's side on the right, under the sun's protection. The back of the ger is reserved for elders, honored guests, and the family altar. The posts symbolize the link with heaven, and it is bad manners to lean against them. A little bag holding herbs to ward off evil spirits is hung from the top. Mongolians never stand or step on the threshold of the door but step over it.

MONGOLIAN WOMEN TODAY

Traditionally clothed women celebrate Naadam in Ulaanbaatar.

Women make up about half the population. In the traditional nomadic society still found in rural areas, women help to milk, feed, and look after the animals, especially when they give birth to their young. They prepare and cook the meat and dairy products and grind the grain. Their important contribution to the functioning of the household gives them status, and they have a say in family matters. The Mongolian constitution guarantees women equal rights with men. Abortion was legalized in 1989.

Before the revolution, women could not choose their husbands nor could they divorce them; they were completely dependent. After the revolution, women were welcomed to every field of education. They could work outside their homes and earn a living, and they could vote. Pregnant women received special benefits at work, in line with the government policy of encouraging larger families. Mongolian women found work as teachers, nurses, doctors, technicians, factory workers, and businesswomen.

With the changeover to a market economy in the 1990s, women were the more severely affected. When state-run factories closed and government departments cut wages and reduced their staffs, more women than men lost their jobs and income. The social-support and health-care systems that had allowed women to work were curtailed, child-care facilities became expensive or were closed, and maternity benefits were reduced. Unemployment and poverty rates continue to remain higher among women.

MARRIAGE IN MONGOLIA

The traditional process of getting married used to be a long, drawn-out affair that took from one to three years and involved matchmakers and the giving of dowries.

An offer was first made by the groom's parents through a matchmaker. After the prospective bride's parents gave a positive reply, both families visited a lama to set a propitious date. Ten days later, the groom's father and

TRADITIONAL FELT MAKING

Felt is a very important product to Mongolians. It is used to cover the ger and to make rugs, saddle pads, and the linings of boots. Felt is made in the fall, and practically everyone takes part in the process. The material is usually made from sheep's wool because the fibers have minute barb-like scales that interlock when they are processed.

The wool is first beaten to clean and loosen the fibers and to mix them up. A very large piece of old felt is placed on the ground and wet. Then three layers of wool are carefully spread on top of it, as evenly as possible, and the wool is then drenched with water. A layer of grass is sprinkled across the top.

Next, the four layers—the old felt with the three layers of new wool—are tightly rolled up around a pole (the grass sprinkled on top prevents the new wool from sticking together). The roll is thoroughly saturated again, then wrapped in leather and tied with leather thongs. Loops at the ends of the pole are attached by ropes to horses. Two riders on horses roll the bundle back and forth until the fibers of the new wool interlock and are tightly compressed, thus forming new felt.

When the roll is unfurled, the new felt is watered down once more and then allowed to dry beneath the sun. The wetting and drying process and the rolling shrinks the felt, making it dense and durable.

A Mongolian couple wed in a traditional marriage ceremony in Ulaanbaatar.

the matchmaker called on the bride's parents with an offering of ceremonial blue silk cloth. Six months after the date was set, the groom visited his intended, and a small party was organized. Six months after the party, gifts were exchanged. On the wedding day, the groom took the bride away to her new home, a new ger built by the groom near the bride's ger. The bride's first duty was to make tea for the guests before the festivities began.

Most modern Mongolians choose their own partner, marry at the Wedding Palace in Ulaanbaatar or state marriage registry, and later celebrate with a feast. Divorce is not common, but the rate is increasing and is 0.28 per 1,000 people.

MODERN AND TRADITIONAL MEDICINE

A Mongolian shaman drinks milk tea after completing a ceremony near Lake Khovsgol.

Mongolians in the past relied on traditional Tibetan and Mongolian medicine and treatments based on local folk beliefs. Modern medical services are now provided by clinics and hospitals. Teaching preventive health care to the people was one of the priorities of the revolutionary government. Infectious diseases—such as smallpox, plague, poliomyelitis, and diphtheria—were major problems caused by poor health habits, infrequent baths, and the difficulty of getting clean drinking water. Great effort has been put into health education, teaching the people better hygiene and how to look after babies and the elderly. Today, the average Mongolian has a life expectancy of 69.9 years, and the infant mortality rate has dropped to 21.1 deaths per 1,000 live births (the United States rate was 5.8 deaths per 1,000 live births in 2017).

While modern medicine has found its place in Mongolia, traditional medicine has been retained. The School of Traditional Medicine in Ulaanbaatar does extensive research on folk medicine practices. It also has an outpatient center for acupuncture, massage, mineral water baths, and mud baths. The school studies the ancient prescriptions and traditional methods of treatment. Special formulas use local medicinal herbs and animal parts such as antelope horns and reindeer antlers. A wolf's intestines are thought to be good for indigestion, and a woodchuck's gallbladder is believed to cure toothache and stomach complaints. Many animals are therefore hunted for their body parts as well as meat. However, there are laws restricting the hunting of rare animals such as the Gobi bear, snow leopard, wild ass, and red wolf. Over four hundred kinds of plants have been found to have medicinal uses.

EDUCATIONAL OPPORTUNITIES

In prerevolutionary days, religion and education were interlinked. There was no secular education. Monasteries took on the task of teaching children Tibetan and how to chant and pray. In higher classes in the monasteries, the older and more privileged children who proved themselves up to the effort were taught

The main building of the Mongolian National University in Ulaanbaatar.

subjects such as philosophy, art, astrology, and medicine. However, the large majority, the children of herders, received no formal education at all.

Following the revolution, the government sought to eradicate illiteracy among both children and adults. The first primary (elementary) school was set up just a month after the government came to power, and more primary schools were promptly built. Boarding schools allowed the children of nomadic families to live comfortably away from home during the school term. The government also started a drive to educate adults. Teachers were sent to homes to teach short-term courses in the evenings. Everyone who could read and write was given the obligation of teaching those who could not. The international agency UNESCO has awarded the N. K. Krupskaya Medal to the Mongolian Institute of Language and Literature of the Academy of Sciences to acknowledge the literacy program's success. It is estimated that 98.4 percent of Mongolians are now literate.

Education is free and compulsory for all children from ages six to fourteen. Children from the age of three may attend kindergarten and learn the basics of reading, writing, and counting. Students aged six to eighteen years attend either secondary schools for university preparation or vocational and technical schools. They learn skills in areas such as construction, manufacturing, transportation, communication, and agriculture that will enable them in time to join the workforce. Since 2008, there has been a transition from an eleven- to a twelve-year schooling system, although a full cycle is not always completed by nomadic adolescents.

In 1922, the first special secondary school was set up to train teachers. There are now several such schools and universities that provide training in dozens of fields, including education, law, and medicine.

The National University of Mongolia was opened in 1942. Some of its departments—such as the State University of Agriculture, National University of Medical Sciences, and Institute of Russian Language—have become separate institutions. As of 2016, Mongolia was home to about one hundred universities, including seventeen state schools.

INTERNET LINKS

https://asiasociety.org/education/women-modern-mongolia
The ways in which women's roles have developed in modern Mongolia are explained by the Asia Society.

https://www.nationalgeographic.org/encyclopedia/yurt
Photographs accompany text about building a yurt, or ger, and the history and modern use of this traditional Mongolian housing.

https://www.ncbi.nlm.nih.gov/pmc/articles/PMC5576166
This article discusses how health-care resources are distributed in Mongolia.

RELIGION

This golden statue of Buddha is in the city of Erdenet.

8

BUDDHISM IS THE PRIMARY RELIGION in Mongolia. More than half of all Mongolians are Buddhists. There are also smaller groups of Muslims and Christians. However, the most ancient and traditional religion in Mongolia is shamanism. It is based on the belief that the spirit world exists in nature. Shamanism is still practiced in Mongolia but is not as prevalent as it once was. During the communist era, religious practices were limited. Today, the constitution of Mongolia guarantees freedom of worship—a legacy handed down from the time of Genghis Khan when the ancient capital of Karakorum was a place where many religions, including shamanism, Christianity, Islam, Confucianism, Taoism, and Buddhism, were practiced side by side.

"During the Soviet era, the party controlled the faith of the people, but they couldn't control their inner devotion."
—Batchunuun Munkhbaatar, Mongolian monk

A Tibetan Buddhist monk reads a religious text.

MONGOLIA'S EARLY RELIGION

Buddhism came to Mongolia very early from the Uyghur people, whose civilization was one of the most advanced in central Asia. Although shamanism was the most influential religion then, the aristocracy, including Genghis Khan, was sympathetic to Buddhism. It was only in the thirteenth century that Buddhism gained real influence. A Tibetan monk who was known by the title of Phagspa Lama became the spiritual head of the country and granted special status to all Buddhist priests, called lamas. They were exempted from military duty and taxes. Buddhism was not widespread, however, because it was the religion of the ruling classes. With the collapse of Kublai Khan's Yuan dynasty, Buddhism lost its influence in Mongolia.

Not until the sixteenth century did Buddhism again become widespread. Mongolian society was in a bad state. Many Mongol leaders were fighting among themselves for power, and people were unhappy and in despair. The rulers felt that a strong religion, such as Buddhism, would strengthen their leadership roles and provide the people with moral fiber. At that time, there was an ongoing rivalry between the Red Hat and Yellow Hat sects of Tibetan Buddhism; each side hoped to gain power through the support of the Mongols. The Chinese Ming dynasty was also anxious to have the Mongols embrace religion, hoping that Buddhism would pacify the restless and warlike Mongols.

In 1578, the Mongol ruler Altan Khan invited the Tibetan religious head, Sonam Gyatso, to Mongolia and gave him the title of Dalai Lama. In return, Altan obtained recognition as the reincarnation of Kublai Khan. These grand gestures reestablished the spiritual links between Mongolia and Tibet. Shamanism and all its practices were effectively banned. The lamas hurriedly adapted shamanist rituals to Buddhist rites to ease the spread of Buddhism.

From then on, Buddhism grew in influence. Translations of large numbers of Buddhist sacred texts from Tibetan into Mongolian helped to make Buddhism accessible to the people. Monasteries were built all over the country and gained

PRAYER WHEELS

Mongolians, like Tibetans, gain spiritual merit by turning prayer wheels. These are hollow cylinders filled with thousands of small paper slips containing prayers. Negative karma and disturbing thoughts are purified by turning the wheel and reciting a mantra. Each clockwise revolution of the cylinder adds to the believer's merit, or good karma, savings account. Prayer wheels are made from different materials, such as leather, metal, wood, and even stone. Small hand-held prayer wheels are easily carried. Large prayer cylinders can be set in different locations, including the ground or the roof of a house. Some are even water powered.

in popularity and influence, mainly because the chief priests were often local princes and other people with wide authority in society. Many lamas were philosophers, scientists, historians, artists, and craftspeople, and the monasteries became centers of learning, influential cultural oases.

Gombordorji Zanabazar, the Javzandamba Khutagt, was a famous reincarnate lama and head of Buddhism in Mongolia. He built the Da Khure monastery in Urga in 1651 and many others. He translated many Buddhist texts. He was also a consummate sculptor and painter of religious statues and scrolls. Seven other Javzandamba Khutagt rulers followed him, but all of them were from Tibet because the Chinese Qing emperors were afraid a Mongol might stir up political trouble. The eighth Javzandamba Khutagt did just that, declaring Mongolia independent of Chinese rule. When he died in 1924, the communist government stopped the search for a successor.

Religious persecution began in 1932. In 1937, under Choibalsan, a former lama who turned revolutionary, more than seventeen thousand monks vanished in purges. Of more than seven hundred monasteries, only four were left standing to serve as museums of the "feudal period." Religious ceremonies were

REINCARNATION

Reincarnation is a basic Buddhist belief that a person or animal will return after death in the form of a different body. Reincarnate lamas are identified by interpreting omens and dreams, and a potential lama is tested. The reincarnate lama Zanabazar was said to be able to recite Tibetan texts at the age of five, without ever having learned that language.

Worshippers gather at Amarbayasgalant monastery in northern Mongolia.

outlawed, except at Gandantegchinlin monastery (also called Gandan) in Ulaanbaatar, until 1990.

THE RETURN OF THE MONASTERY

In the early 1990s the decline of communist rule led to the restoration of religious practices. About two thousand lamas established small communities at the sites of some 120 former monasteries, and many monasteries that were damaged during the persecution of the 1930s were restored.

The three big monasteries in Mongolia are the Gandan monastery in Ulaanbaatar, the Erdene Zuu in Karakorum, and the Amarbayasgalant monastery near Darkhan. Gandan, the largest and most important center of Buddhism, was built in 1838. Its library houses thousands of rare books and manuscripts in Tibetan, Mongolian, and other languages. The monastery is the headquarters of the Asian Buddhist Conference for Peace, an organization made up of members from many Asian countries.

THE SPIRIT WORLD

Shamanism, characterized by supernatural insights of a shaman, or priest, was very important in the spiritual life of the people until the sixteenth century. During the rule of Genghis Khan, its practice played a big role. The people believed that Genghis received his authority to rule from Tengri, the supreme sky god. There were many shamans in Genghis's court who acted as intermediaries between the people and the unseen spirit world. A chief shaman could determine, with the help of his bond to the spirit world, when it was time to break camp, where the khan's camp should go next, and when it was the right time to go to war. The shaman could make countless other big and small decisions. The shaman helped to cure illnesses, drive away evil spirits, find lost animals, and make predictions, and was consulted for a favorable date on which to hold an important event such as cutting a child's hair for the first time, doing business, or getting married.

Mongolia shares a tradition of shamanism with many other hunting-gathering cultures in central Asia and North America. A shaman most often comes from a family with a tradition of shamanism. Both men and women can be shamans. A person destined to become a shaman is usually identified by some uncommon behavior such as fainting spells or visions. The candidate takes years to learn to communicate with the spirits. The process includes prolonged fasts, living like a hermit, and interpreting dreams and visions, his own and those of others.

"The world is alive, everything is alive. The plants, animals, rocks, and water all have spirits. These spirits must be respected and cared for or else the land would become hostile or barren. Therefore, protection and balance of one's environment is of utmost importance."
—Shamanic wisdom from the Circle of Tengerism

Against a stormy landscape, a shaman performs a ritual.

MYTHS AND SUPERSTITIONS

Many myths and beliefs connected with shamanism explain the relationship between the heavens and the people, the creation of the world, and the role of nature. It is believed that there are three worlds: the heavenly upper world ruled by Tengri, the earthly middle world inhabited by people, and the subterranean lower world ruled over by Erleg Khan (ER-leg khan), where the souls of the dead await reincarnation. The sky is male, and the earth is female.

Many folk beliefs are connected with the countryside, and these are based on a belief in the sacredness of mountains, lakes, and other natural objects. Mongolians are superstitious, believing in charms, strange events, and miracles. Everyday objects may possess magical qualities. For example, the stirrup is important in a horse-riding society, and when a man leaves on a long trip, milk is sprinkled on it to bless it. Many superstitions concern animals. Because the peacock is sacred, Mongolian homes often display peacock feathers to purify the room. Crows and snakes are believed to cast spells, and a goose is considered capable of breaking a stirrup if the rider does something bad to the bird. It is believed that one's very own star shines when one is born and disappears from the sky when one dies. If one is very lucky or has a happy life, it is due to one's lucky star.

OTHER RELIGIONS

Muslims make up about 3 percent of the total population. Most are Kazakhs living in Bayan-Olgi in the west. The Muslims also suffered during the persecution of religion under the communists, when many mosques were closed or destroyed, as were the Buddhist monasteries. Some have been reopened or are being rebuilt. Christians form about 2.2 percent of the population. A law passed in 1993 regarding state and church relations restricted religious activities largely in favor of Buddhism. This law made it difficult for Christian churches to organize themselves, though many of the laws have been repealed or relaxed after constitutional challenges in court. However, some religious groups are still affected by difficult government stipulations.

OVOO

An ovoo (AW-waw) is a sacred shrine set on a mountain slope or near a lake or river in open land. It looks like a pile of stones or rocks placed in the shape of a pyramid. Bottles of vodka, bits of tobacco, colored scraps of cloth, and even money or candy are often placed on the ovoo as an offering to the gods. When a person comes across an ovoo, he usually walks clockwise around it three times. Then he adds some kind of offering to the collection already there.

Sometimes a small religious ceremony is held at an ovoo. Lamas say prayers accompanied by libations, or the pouring of liquor (usually airag), on the shrine, and people make offerings. There is usually some feasting followed by a small festival of sports. This ritual usually celebrates the coming of spring. It is also held to pray for good weather, abundant rainfall, plentiful pastureland for the animals, and successful hunting.

This ceremony, which was prohibited during the communist era, has made a comeback with the greater freedom of democracy since the 1990s.

INTERNET LINKS

https://www.goyotravel.com/5-enigmatic-monasteries-mongolia

This tour group website has a page dedicated to "Mongolia's Magical Monasteries."

https://sacredsites.com/asia/mongolia/mongolian_shamanism.html

Sites that are sacred in Mongolian shamanism are featured through a series of photographs.

https://www.youtube.com/watch?v=gqNZvOkdQqA

A study of Mongolian shamanism is presented in this video.

LANGUAGE

Mongolian is often written using the Cyrillic alphabet.

9

"If you endeavor,
fate endeavors."
—Mongolian saying

THE MONGOLIAN LANGUAGE, LIKE its culture, has been shaped by the many historical influences that have impacted the country and its people over the centuries. This is especially evident in the written form of the language. The written Mongolian of today dates back to the thirteenth century. It has survived many changes over time, and like all languages, it has kept the elements that work best. Another important form of communication is nonverbal language. This unspoken language of gestures and body language has a long history of usage in Mongolia often tied into etiquette.

SPEAKING MONGOLIAN

The languages and dialects spoken in Mongolia have been influenced by the country's history, geography, and varied cultures. Ninety-five percent of the people in Mongolia and those living in Inner Mongolia, which is part

A VARIETY OF WORDS

The Mongolian language contains a great variety of words that can describe the same or similar things. There are several words for grasses and animals and many variations of such words. Mori *is a gelding.* Xiimori *is a flying magic horse, and the word also means "healthy."* Morisaitai *means "fortunate," or a person who owns a good horse. The* morin khuur *is a traditional horse-head fiddle.*

of China, speak Mongolian. It is also spoken by groups of people living in other provinces of China and in the Russian Federation. Worldwide, seven million people speak Mongolian, of which 56 percent live in Mongolia.

Mongolian is part of the Altaic family of languages that is spoken over a wide area from Turkey in the west to the Pacific Ocean in the east. Many different dialects are spoken by the various Mongolian tribes, but there are basically four main ones. Khalkha is the dialect spoken by most Mongolians and on which the official language is based. The other three main dialect groups are the Western or Oirat dialects, spoken in the western parts of the country; the Buryat dialect, spoken in the north around Lake Baikal; and the Inner Mongolian dialects of the south.

WRITING MONGOLIAN

When writing became necessary for administrative and religious missionary work, the Mongols developed their written script by borrowing characters from other people. Thus, their script has changed many times.

The written language in use today dates back to the thirteenth century. According to Mongolian history, Genghis Khan decreed that there be devised a proper written Mongolian language. After conquering the Uyghur people, he commanded his captive Uyghur adviser, Tatatungo, to adapt the ancient Uyghur script to the Mongolian language. The long, stringlike letters were connected by continuous lines from top to bottom and read from left to right.

When Kublai Khan was in power, he wanted a new written language to unite the many different languages of his far-flung empire. He ordered the Tibetan

OTHER LANGUAGES IN MONGOLIA

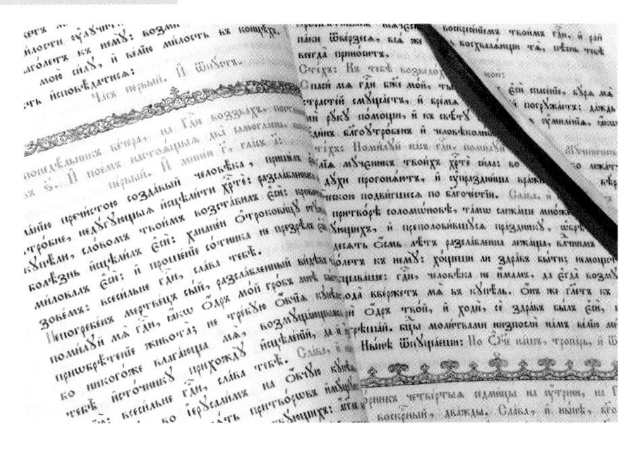

Many Mongolians, having been educated in Russia, are also fluent in Russian. English is becoming a popular second language as Mongolians seek to engage more in the global market. Because a large number of Mongolians living abroad are concentrated in Korea, a number of Mongolians have learned Korean. There are also some German speakers in Mongolia. Kazakh and Tuvan are two Turkic languages known by a small segment of the population. There are Kazakh speakers in western Mongolia, and a small group that lives along the border of the Tuva Republic in Russia speaks Tuvan.

scholar and monk Phagspa Lama to devise a new alphabet. The Square script, with square-shaped letters, emerged for a short period of time. It was based on the Tibetan and Indian alphabets and was written from top to bottom. It was the official script of the Yuan dynasty. When Kublai's rule ended, the script fell into disuse, although examples remain in inscriptions in temples, seals, and title pages of ancient books.

In the seventeenth century, two other handwritings were invented. Both the Clear script, which tried to bring the written language closer to the spoken language, and the Horizontal Square script, based on an ancient form of Indian writing, could transcribe and record words in Mongolian, Tibetan, and Sanskrit. In the early twentieth century, yet one more, the Vaghintara script, was invented for transcribing Russian words into Mongolian. All three scripts were short-lived.

While Mongolia was under Soviet influence, the Mongolian script was replaced by Cyrillic, an alphabet that was developed in the ninth century based on Greek characters and was the foundation of the Russian script. Cyrillic writing cannot represent some of the sounds in spoken Mongolian. Still, the

The current flag of Mongolia was adopted in 1992.

Mongolian written language today is based on Cyrillic, with modifications. The alphabet has twenty-six letters, and it is written from the top down, left to right. Since Mongolia declared its independence from Soviet influence, there arose popular interest in reviving the traditional script of Genghis Khan. In 1990, the government resolved to reintroduce the Mongolian script by 1994. This plan has yet to be fully implemented, but some schools are teaching it to some degree.

THE PRESS AND BROADCASTING

The beginnings of Mongolian-language newspapers date to the end of the nineteenth century and early twentieth century, when both the Soviet Union and China became more interested in increasing their influence in Mongolia. A Mongolian newspaper was published in the early 1900s by the Mongolian literati who wanted to liberate their country from Chinese rule. To counter the influence of the paper, China-inspired journals in Mongolian were distributed in Mongolia but found few readers. During the revolution, Mongolian revolutionaries published their own paper, the *Mongolian Truth* (Mongoliin Unen), which became the voice of the Mongolian People's Revolutionary Party. Now known as *Unen* (Truth), it is the oldest paper in the nation. There are eleven daily newspapers, of which *Onoodor* is the largest. *UB Post* is the leading English-language news outlet in the country.

With greater freedom and democracy, Mongolia now has about one hundred newspapers and more than eighty magazines and other publications. Papers and journals produced by trade unions, the army, and scientific, literary, artistic, and cultural organizations have also proliferated.

The Mongolian state-run radio began broadcasting in 1934. It broadcasted government programs, as well as traditional folk music, epics, and Western classical music. In 2005, state-run broadcasting outlets became public service

THE SOYOMBO SCRIPT AND SYMBOL

The Soyombo (SOH-yom-bo) script was introduced by Gombordorji Zanabazar in 1686. It was such a complex and ornamental script that it became impractical for wide use. Instead, it was limited to religious applications in prayers and religious texts. What has remained of this script, however, is the Soyombo symbol, which has been adopted as the Mongolian national emblem of freedom and independence. It is depicted in the state emblem and in the national flag.

At the very top of the Soyombo symbol is a flame symbolizing blossoming, revival, and the continuation of the family. The three points of the flame symbolize the past, present, and future prosperity of the people. Below the flame is the sun and the crescent moon, symbolizing the origin of the Mongolian people. The flame, sun, and moon together express the determination that the Mongolian people may always live and prosper.

Next come some geometric forms—triangles and rectangles. The triangles express the wish for freedom and independence, while the horizontal rectangles symbolize honesty, justice, and nobility. The broader, vertical rectangles symbolize the walls of a fortress. In the middle of the geometric section of the emblem are two intertwined fish, which resemble the Chinese yin-yang symbol and signify natural complements like male and female or night and day. In Mongolian folklore, fish never close their eyes and are therefore vigilant creatures. This part of the Soyombo emblem expresses the belief that the Mongolian people will stay united so that they are stronger than the walls of a fortress.

providers. Radio Ulaanbaatar, a privately owned station, offers English-speaking programs and Western music. In Mongolia, the radio is a very important source of information and entertainment, especially in rural areas. A portable radio is the herder's inseparable companion. Now there are almost seventy radio stations that broadcast in Mongolian, English, and Russian.

The first television station in Mongolia was started by the government in 1967. For a time, programming consisted largely of Russian movies dubbed into Mongolian, and locally produced documentaries, newscasts, and sports

"*Khatun* (queen) is one of the most authoritative and magnificent words in the Mongolian language. It conveys regality, stateliness, and great strength. If something resists breaking no matter how much pressure is applied, it is described as *khatun*." —Jack Weatherford, author

programs, especially wrestling, which is still extremely popular. Now a wide choice of television programs are beamed to all the aimag capitals and to more than fifty other administrative centers. There are more than 130 broadcast channels. Even remote ger dwellers can plug their televisions and satellite dishes into a solar panel and watch a Hollywood blockbuster.

NAMES AND TITLES

Mongolian names usually consist of two names. The first is the patronymic name, or the father's name, often in a possessive form; the second is the given name. So, former prime minister Yumjaagiin Tsedenbal's given name is Tsedenbal. His father is Yumjaag. People are usually called by their given name. When there is a title indicating a person's rank or age, it comes after the name. For example, Mr. Tsedenbal is Tsedenbal *guai* (GOO-ai).

UNSPOKEN COMMUNICATION

Mongolians use the right hand to gesture with and to take things. When receiving a gift, food, or snuff, it is proper to do it with both hands; the right

Former US secretary of state John Kerry greets archers during the 2016 Naadam Festival in Ulaanbaatar.

hand only may be used but with the left hand touching the right elbow as if in support. Mongolians beckon someone with the fingers of the right hand, a little outstretched, palm facing down.

In the city, a handshake is acceptable. In a traditional greeting between two people of different ages or status, the one younger or lower in status gently supports the forearms of the other. This greeting is also used to show respect to elders during the Lunar New Year. It is impolite to point with one finger; all the fingers are used. Other taboos are crossing one's legs and kicking someone, even accidentally. An immediate apology is due. It is rude to stare directly into the eyes of an elder. Women cover their mouths in a gesture of modesty when laughing. In greetings, an inquiry about health is added as well as a question concerning a seasonal activity, for example, "How was the harvest?" It is considered good manners to ask nomadic herders about their animals.

INTERNET LINKS

http://thediplomat.com/2016/06/media-in-mongolia
This Asian newspaper has a video that examines the state of the media in Mongolia.

https://www.omniglot.com/writing/mongolian.htm
Written and spoken Mongolian is discussed on this website that includes a video on pronunciation.

http://www.theubpost.mn
The *UB Post* is the leading English-language newspaper in Mongolia.

ARTS

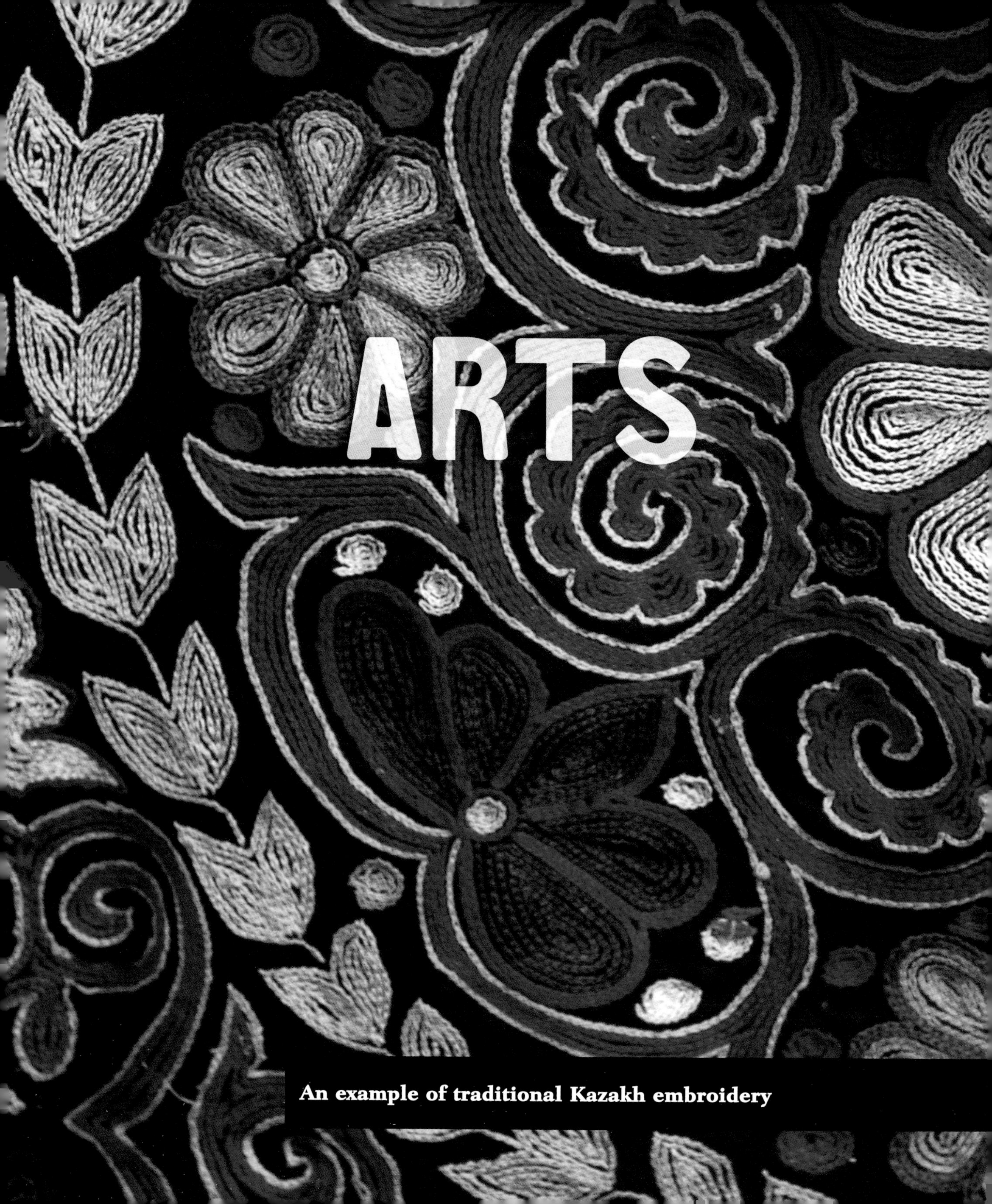

An example of traditional Kazakh embroidery

10

MONGOLIANS HAVE BEEN LARGELY nomadic for thousands of years, yet they have a deep cultural heritage that is just as old. Since they have been a society on the move, this may not translate into permanent buildings or monuments. However, Mongolians have expressed their artistic creativity through everyday useful articles—such as boots, saddles, and hunting tools—that are well made and uniquely decorated. Later, skilled artisans created art that served religion, such as paintings, statutes, monasteries, and temples. Also deeply rooted in Mongolia's history is the art of storytelling. Before written Mongolian evolved, a strong oral tradition preserved the history of the country. Traveling storytellers crisscrossed the mountains and steppes, performing in return for food, money, and shelter.

"Everything is faded like raincloud, but photography is left like earth."

—Mongolian saying

THE ORAL TRADITION

The art of reciting an epic poem is very exacting, requiring great concentration, an excellent memory, and acting and oratorical skills. Often hundreds or thousands of verses have to be learned to recite just one poem. The tradition of reciting epic poems dates back to the days when the Mongols were a collection of tribes, and storytellers reciting tribal history were welcomed performers. One of the most ancient epics is the story of Huuheldei Mergen Khan, a great hunter who shoots a magic deer. Another is the story of the hero Geser, sent to earth to combat evil.

These ancient megaliths depicting flying deer are found throughout Mongolia.

EARLY MATERIAL CULTURE

Mongolia is said to have been inhabited from very early times, and many scholars believe that humans from this part of central Asia migrated north and east, crossed the land bridge that used to span the Bering Strait, and populated North America—the earliest stock of the first Americans! Stone tools dating back some five hundred thousand years have been found in Mongolia. The oldest evidence of some sort of art and culture comes from the Bronze Age, which goes back to approximately 3000 BCE or earlier in Mongolia.

The people, though nomadic, carved and shaped rectangular stone monuments called "reindeer stones" and placed them upright in valleys, open grasslands, and hillsides, probably as markers of sacred sites or graves. These were possibly the beginnings of ovoo, or shaman shrines. The stones are from 3 to 13 feet (1 to 4 m) high and bear images of celestial bodies such as the sun or the moon in the upper section, graceful running and jumping deer in the middle section, and images of tools and weapons, including knives, swords, hooks, bows and quivers of arrows, and axes in the bottom section.

The artists of the sixth to eighth centuries CE had greater carving ability. They created lifelike statues of people, complete with clothing of that period and the weapons and tools they used. This representational tradition continued into the thirteenth century.

The Mongolian artist Balduugiin Sharav painted this scene, titled *One Day in the Life of Mongolia.*

ART IN MONGOLIA

Painting in Mongolia dates back to the eighth century CE with the paintings of the Uyghurs. Later painting took on a religious significance and had Buddhist themes. The paintings were done on cloth, using mineral and vegetable dyes, and were often framed with silk. Traditionally they had red, white, or black backgrounds. Some religious "paintings" were appliqués created by sewing pieces of silk and other fabrics onto larger pieces of cloth. These silk paintings decorated many temples and palaces. Religious paintings hang in many homes today.

Mongolian painting next took on a form called Mongol *zurag* (ZOO-rug), which is distinctive in almost completely filling the space, the use of certain colors, and a two-dimensional, flat style. These depict the simple life and traditions of the people. The best-known painter of this school is Balduugiin Sharav (1869–1939). His most famous work is *One Day in the Life of Mongolia*. Landscape artist L. Gavaa and portrait painters O. Tsevegjav (1915–1975) and U. Yadamsuren (1905–1986) further developed the style of Mongol zurag.

GREAT WRITERS

Noyon Khutagt Danzanravjaa and Vanchinbalyn Injinash were two significant nineteenth-century Mongolian writers. Noyon Khutagt Danzanravjaa wrote many religious treatises but was more popular for the more than four hundred nonreligious poems and songs he composed, including "Fair Wind," "The Charming," and "The Four Seasons of the Year." Vanchinbalyn Injinash's most famous work was the Koke Sudur, *or "Blue Chronicle," a fictional version of Mongol history extolling humanistic and patriotic ideals.*

Ancient artwork of the deity Tara

Sculpture had religious themes. Zanabazar (1635—1723), Mongolia's most famous sculptor and painter, created many religious statues and paintings. He learned bronze casting from the Tibetans, and his works include bronze statues of Buddhist deities, especially Tara, the deity of compassion.

WRITTEN WORKS

Mongolian heroic epics—tales of war and empire, myths of origin, histories of the Great Khans—were written down more than 750 years ago. The earliest and most important of these stories is *The Secret History of the Mongols*, about the origin of the greatest Mongol ever, Genghis Khan. After the decline of the Mongol Empire, the tradition of storytelling continued into the fifteenth and sixteenth centuries, with stories about the power struggles among the many tribal princes.

The seventeenth century saw the rise of philosophical and didactic poetry by the lamas. This coincided with the prominence of Buddhism and continued until the nineteenth century. Chinese poetry and stories were translated during the period spanning the seventeenth to the nineteenth centuries, including Chinese classics such as *Dream of the Red Chamber, Romance of the Three Kingdoms*, and *The Water Margin*.

Modern Mongol literature emerged during the revolution as writers became exposed to Western and world literature, in tandem with Eastern literature, and drew inspiration from both sources. Revolutionary and nationalistic feelings were common themes of their poems, novels, and plays. Writers also translated world literature, making it possible for the people to read works by Lu Xun, William Shakespeare, Leo Tolstoy, Alexandre Dumas, and Rabindranath Tagore in the Mongolian language. Modern Mongolian writers of importance are Dashdorjiin Natsagdorj (1906—1937), often described as the father of contemporary Mongolian literature, Sodnombaljiriin Buyannemeh (1901—1937), Tsendiin Damdinsuren (1908—1986), and Donroviin Namdag (1911—1984).

This monument of the writer Danzanravjaa stands at the entrance to the Museum of Sainshand.

PHYSICAL STRUCTURES

Although nomadic, the Mongols built towns and villages. There is archaeological evidence of more than two hundred ancient towns in Mongolia. These were a combination of movable homes and settlements and more permanent structures.

Karakorum, an old Uyghur site on the banks of the Orkhon River, was first settled by Genghis Khan in 1220. It served as his headquarters. A palace for Genghis's son Odegei was completed at Karakorum in 1235. The city was divided into sectors for administrators, traders, craftsmen, artisans, and private individuals. The palace's main hall had a green enamel brick floor, and the roof tiles were green and red enamel. Around the palace were the residences of the princes and courtiers. Karakorum was destroyed by a Ming invasion in 1388. Today, only one of the original four statuary turtles believed to protect the city from floods stands as a lonely sentinel.

Visitors walk among the ruins of the historic town of Karakorum.

There were many temples and monasteries when Mongolia was the center of the Buddhist world, and these were influenced by both the East and the West. The famed Erdene Zuu monastery, built in 1586, was constructed on a square plan. A brick wall topped with 108 stupas, or pagodas, spaced evenly apart, enclosed it. The huge Buddhist complex included sixty temples and housed ten thousand resident lamas.

THE SECRET HISTORY OF THE MONGOLS

This text describes the origin of the Mongols, particularly the birth and rise of Genghis Khan, the first ruler of Mongolia to unite the nomadic tribes of central Asia. It is told in more than thirty stories and over two hundred poems and songs that are part fact and part fable. A sample follows:

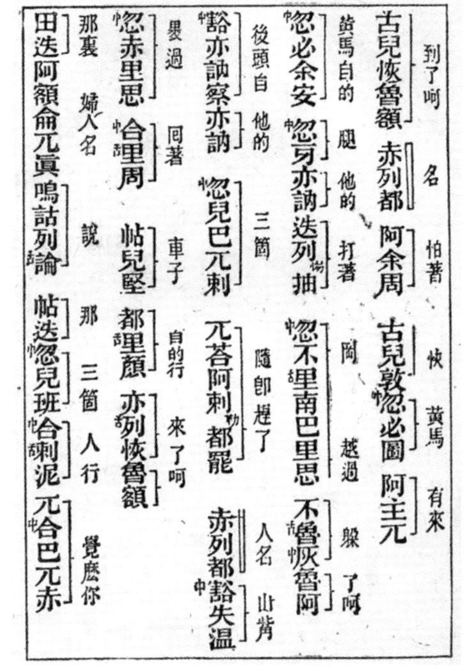
到了呵 名 怕著 快 黃馬 有來
古兒恢魯額 赤列都 阿余周 古兒敦忽必圖 阿主兀
黃馬 自的 腿 他的 打著 岡 越過 躲 了呵
忽必余安 忽牙亦訥 迭列 抽 忽不里南巴里思 不魯恢魯阿
後頭自 他的 三箇 隨即 趕了 人名 山背
豁亦訥察亦訥 忽兒巴兀剌 兀答阿剌 都罷 赤列都豁失溫
要過 同著 車子 自的行 來了呵
忽赤里思 合里周 帖兒堅 都里顏 亦列恢魯額
那裏 婦人名 說 那 三箇 人 行 覺麽你
田迭阿額侖兀眞嗚詁列論 帖迭忽兒班合剌泥 兀合巴兀赤

In the beginning Blue-Gray Wolf and Beautiful Doe came from across the sea and settled at the source of the Onon River in northeast Mongolia, near Burkhan Khaldun, the "Mountain of the Shaman Spirit." Beautiful Doe gave birth to a son, Batachikhan, whose descendants pastured herds and hunted game on the slopes of the mountain.

In the twenty-first generation a boy was born with a clot of blood in his right fist. He was the future Chinggis [Genghis] Khan. His father, Yesugei the Brave, was the chief of one of the Mongol tribes. At that time, there was much feuding and rivalry among the many tribes. One day, while hunting, Yesugei met a woman and her husband from another tribe and abducted her, making her his wife. Ho'elun bore him five children—four sons and a daughter. The eldest was Temujin, "blacksmith."

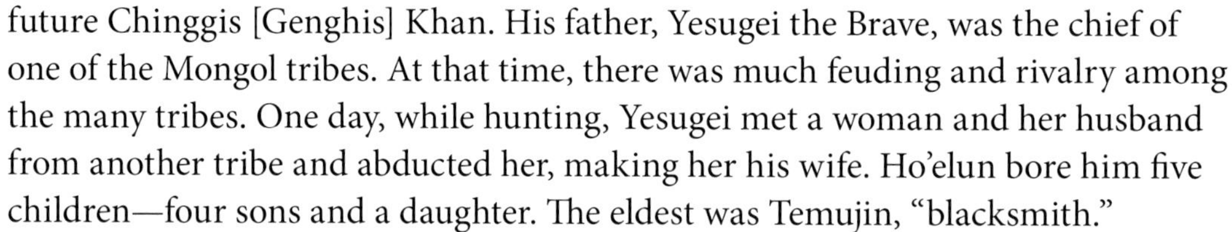

Temujin, at the age of nine, lost his father who was poisoned by a rival tribe, the Tatars. The family then lived on the banks of the river. The other tribes captured Temujin, afraid that he would become a leader when he came of age. They made him wear a heavy wooden yoke around his neck.

Eventually Temujin escaped, and he and his family lived like outlaws on Burkhan Khaldun. He gathered followers and grew in power. In 1206, at a great assembly of all the Mongol tribes, when he was about forty years old, Temujin was proclaimed Chinggis Khan—"strong ruler."

ARTS AND CRAFTS

In modern times, everyday objects and work tools are embellished with silver, embroidery, carvings, and appliqué work. Saddles, stirrups, and tools associated with horses are often carefully crafted, beautiful works of art. Intricate designs are carved on furniture, ger doors, hunting weapons, work tools, and musical instruments.

There are lavishly designed gold and silver accessories and wonderfully embroidered pouches and cases for carrying snuff bottles, pipes, and eating sets. Traditional clothing is also enriched with finely worked gold and silver jewelry.

MUSIC IN MONGOLIA

Mongolians love music and have developed distinctive styles. There are two basic kinds of songs, the short and the long. Short songs are usually lively and tell of everyday activities, love, and nature. Long songs are more philosophical, dealing with love, the meaning of life, and the relationship between people and

Musicians in Ulaanbaatar perform on traditional instruments.

nature. Long songs are formal and are often performed at important functions, festivities, and ceremonies. They are harder to sing, and some songs have as many as twenty thousand lines.

A special way of singing in Mongolia is called *khoomi* (KHAW-me), or throat singing. Through careful control of the throat, tongue, mouth, and nose, khoomi singers can create unique sounds that are quite unlike conventional Western singing. Professional khoomi singers come from certain regions where there is a strong tradition of this music. The Chandmani district of Khovd aimag in western Mongolia is the home of khoomi. Throat singing produces many different sounds by forcing air through the mouth and throat and by using the tongue to form a resonant chamber in the mouth. Khoomi is a tradition shared with the neighboring Tuva Republic. Many other people have an interest in throat singing. Among them are Australians, Japanese, Americans, Canadians, Finns, and Irish.

Among the musical folk instruments are the *morin khuur* (MAW-rin kher), a two-stringed fiddle with a head shaped like a horse's head. The bow is made from the hair of a horse's tail, like Western violin bows. It creates a beautiful yet mournful sound that comes closest to expressing the deep feelings of the heart. This instrument often accompanies the long, loving songs that describe the beauty of the Mongolian countryside.

Some other instruments are the *shudrag* (SHOOD-rug), a three-stringed lute with a long neck and a round wooden sound box covered with skin; the *limbe* (LIM-beh), a flute made of a simple, straight bamboo tube with at least eight finger holes; the *yoching* (YAW-ching), a board zither with two rows of fourteen metal strings stretched over a board and struck with two hammers; and the *yatag* (YAH-tug), a plucked stringed instrument with ten to fourteen strings stretched across a long sound box.

Mongolian theater, opera, and ballet are popular and have all been influenced by the Russian forms of these arts. While Russian operas are beloved, there are also Mongolian operas. The first known Mongolian opera was written by Dashdorjiin Natsagdorj. Performers were mostly trained in the Soviet Union. The National Academic Theatre of Opera and Ballet of Mongolia in Ulaanbaatar—first established in 1963— offers more than one hundred performances a year.

This folk troupe performs a cultural dance in Ulaanbaatar.

Folk dancing can be seen during celebrations. The most famous dance is the *bielgee* (BEE-el-gee) or dance of the body, typically performed by a slender girl to music. The dance usually consists of head and hand movements alone, since this dance was originally performed in gers where there was little space.

INTERNET LINKS

http://www.mongoliamusic.weebly.com/instruments.html
Mongolia's unique musical instruments are demonstrated on this website.

http://www.tibetheritagefund.org/pages/projects/mongolia/mongolian-architecture.php
This website explains the building materials and methods traditionally used in Mongolian architecture.

LEISURE

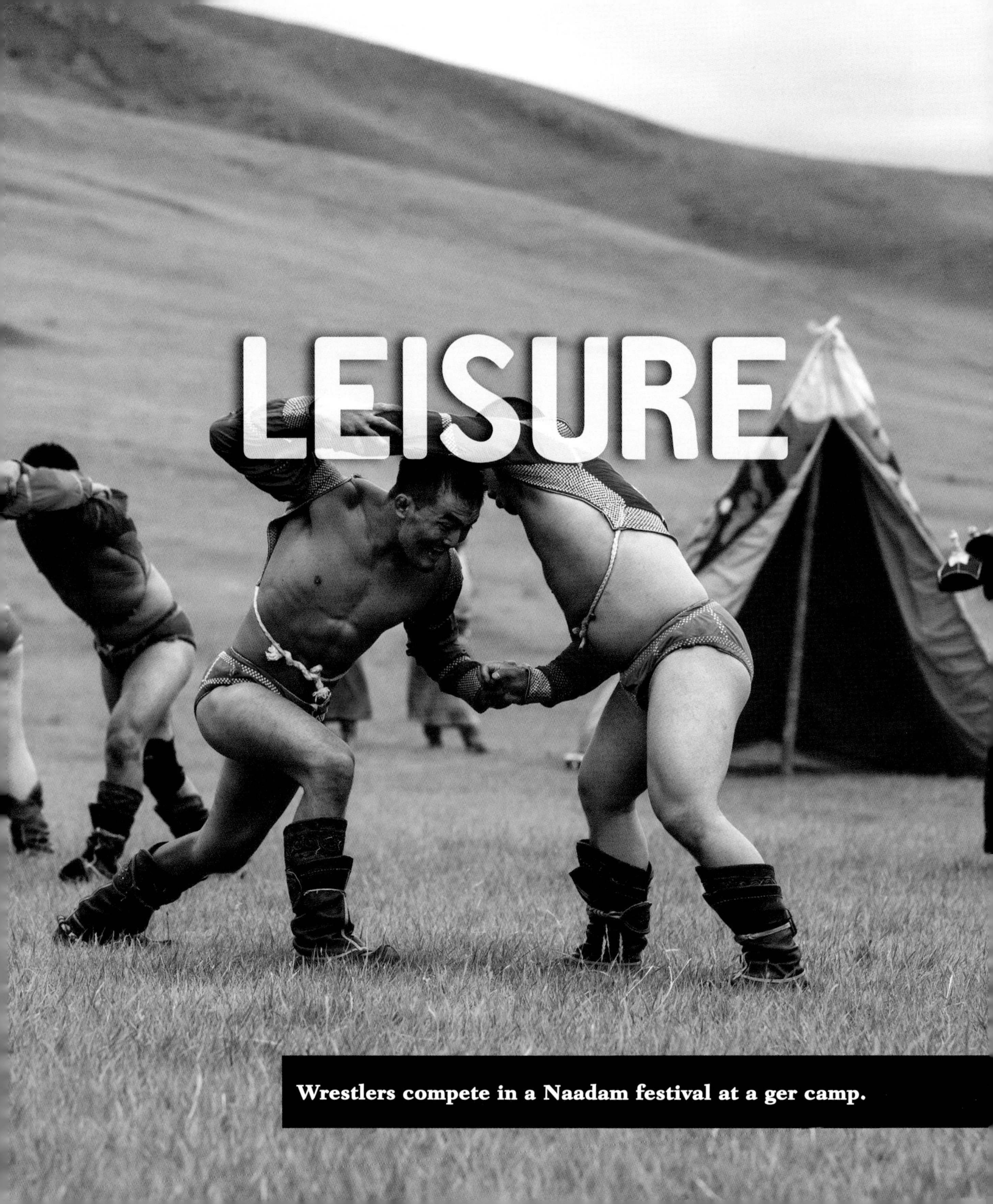

Wrestlers compete in a Naadam festival at a ger camp.

11

LEISURE TIME FOR MONGOLIANS IS tied to the pastoral traditions of their history, drawing on their connection to the land and to animals. Their most important and time-revered leisure activities are sports and other athletic competitions such as wresting, archery, and horse racing. The ancient pastime of telling folktales has been passed down through the generations. Mongolians hunt game for food and as a pastime. More contemporary ways of enjoying leisure time—such as going to concerts, movies, ballets, operas, and even shopping—have evolved with the modern age. But spending time in the wide outdoors brings many Mongolians, especially urban dwellers, back to their cultural roots.

"In Mongolian culture, Khutulun is remembered by the sport in which she so excelled. These days when Mongolian men wrestle, they wear a sort of long-sleeved vest that is open in the front to prove to their opponents they don't have breasts. It's a tribute to the woman wrestler who was never defeated."

—Linda Rodriguez McRobbie, *Princesses Behaving Badly: Real Stories from History—Without the Fairy Tale Endings*

Young Mongolians practice archery.

ATHLETIC COMPETITIONS

Horse racing, wrestling, and archery are known as the three "manly" sports in Mongolia, although girls and women take part in both horse racing and archery. Practically the entire country turns out to watch competitions in these three sports during the national Naadam festival that takes place each year in July.

Riding skills are necessary in a pastoral and nomadic society, with families moving with the seasons. Mongolians do not learn riding for sport but as an essential life skill. Children learn to ride a horse almost as soon as they start to walk. Practically every Mongolian knows how to ride, and they are recognized as excellent equestrians.

"The Mongol, above all things, is not a farmer … On the ground, he is as awkward as a duck out of water … The back of a pony is his real home … He will do wonderfully well any work which keeps him in the saddle." —Roy Chapman Andrews, *Across Mongolian Plains*

Mongolian boys are also taught to wrestle from an early age. The most promising ones are trained in special camps. They learn all the classic moves and throws, the correct wrestler's stance (said to be a combination of the posture of a lion and the outspread wings of a bird in flight), and the victorious "eagle dance."

Archery, the third manly sport, is practiced by men and women alike, using the same type of equipment and technique. The Mongolian bow is double-curved, and made of horn, sinew, bark, and wood. Arrowheads are made of bone. The string is drawn back with the aid of a thumb ring made of leather.

ANCIENT PASTIMES

The game of "shooting bones" has been around since the time of Genghis Khan. There are several variations, but all are played with the anklebones of a lamb. Each side of the bone is shaped differently and has a name—horse, camel, goat, or sheep. A favorite form of the game uses sets of eight or twelve

HORSE SKILLS

Mongolians are skillful horse riders owing to their long history of nomadic life. They often ride standing nearly upright in short stirrups. An urgha *(OOR-ga)—a willow or bamboo pole about 30 feet (9 m) long with a rope attached to the tip—is used to lasso the animals. Mongolian herders allow their horses to roam freely, keeping them semiwild. Thus, they have to corral, lasso, and break in the animals each time they use them.*

bones that are "shot" at a target, two at a time, with the aid of a special wooden paddle. The winner is the player with the greatest number of bones at the end of the game.

"Catching horses" is another popular pastime among Mongolians. In this game, boys in one group separate a wild horse from the rest of the herd and then chase it back at high speed. Another group of boys waits for the horse to gallop by and tries to lasso it. This exciting game develops very important skills among Mongolian boys.

Anklebone shooting at the Naadam Festival in Ulaanbaatar

THE PURSUIT OF GAME

Mongolians love hunting, which for them has a practical purpose. They shoot various game such as deer, rabbits, and marmots for their meat, pelts, and other valuable parts. They also kill other animals that prey on livestock. Hunting used to be carried out with spears or bows and arrows. Today, traps and guns have largely taken their place.

Wolves are a favorite target because they attack livestock, their pelts bring a good price, and their intestines are valued for their medicinal uses. Marmots are also common prey almost everywhere on the steppes.

LEISURE-TIME ACTIVITIES

Going to the movies is becoming increasingly popular, particularly among the young. Most of the films used to be from the Soviet Union and Eastern European countries, but Hollywood films have taken an increasing hold on Mongolian moviegoers. American Westerns are very popular in Mongolia, possibly because of the scenes of wide-open spaces and cowboys on horses. Mongolians turn to television and radio to occupy much of their leisure time, especially during the winter.

Young Mongolians love listening to Western popular music, including jazz and rock. There are also a number of homegrown Mongolian rock and even heavy metal groups.

Window-shopping is an increasing leisure activity in the towns, as people enjoy looking at the varied merchandise, such as Western-style clothing. There are many recreational spas at hot-water springs that are believed to have curative effects. Naturally, the outdoors is very important even for those who live in cities, who greatly enjoy going to the countryside to visit friends and

Young Mongolians enjoy a concert.

MONGOLIAN CHESS

The game of chess is a very old and traditional pastime in Mongolia and is extremely popular, as is checkers. Mongolian chess is played on a chessboard similar to the Western chessboard, but the game pieces are different and reflect Mongolia's pastoral and nomadic lifestyle. The king, pawn, knight, castle, bishop, and queen are replaced by the khan, boy, horse, cart, camel, and lion or dog.

relatives. Those who can afford it retreat with their families to country gers or small cabins in the summer.

ATHLETIC GAMES

Mongolians are very sports oriented because their nomadic traditions keep them outdoors and physically active. The most popular games are basketball, volleyball, soccer, and gymnastics. The capital city, Ulaanbaatar, has a soccer stadium and an indoor coliseum. Motorcycle racing, bicycling, hang gliding, and mountain climbing draw many enthusiasts. Skiing and ice-skating on frozen rivers and lakes are extremely popular winter sports.

Sports are nurtured in schools as an important part of the curriculum. This importance is reflected in the National Games, a nationwide competition of several winter and summer sports organized by the country's sports clubs and associations.

Medal winner Nyam-Ochir Sainjargal at the 2012 Summer Olympics.

Mongolians have also done well in international competitions. Their athletes take part in the Asian Games, the Olympic Games, and various world championships. They have done very well in freestyle wrestling, winning four silvers and four bronzes in that event at the Olympic Games over the twenty-year period from 1968 to 1988. In the 2008 Summer Olympics in Beijing, Mongolia took home two gold and two silver medals. In the 2012 summer games in London, Mongolia won two silver and three bronze medals. One silver and one bronze medal were taken home from the 2016 summer games in Rio de Janeiro.

AN OLD FOLKTALE

How the Camel Lost Its Antlers and Its Tail

Once upon a time, the camel had beautiful antlers on its head and a long, luxurious tail. The deer, on the other hand, had a bald head and the horse, a thin and bedraggled tail. Both the deer and the horse envied the camel for its wonderful good looks.

One day, when the camel went down to the water to drink, it met the deer. "Could I borrow your antlers for a day?" the deer asked the camel. "There is a big celebration tonight, and I am ashamed of going with my bald head." The camel, being generous, agreed, on the condition that the deer would come to the water's edge the next day and return the antlers.

As the happy deer went on its way, holding its head up high to show off the antlers it had just gained, it met the horse. "Where did you get those antlers?" asked the horse. The deer told the horse everything. The horse thought this would be an excellent chance to fool the camel and get its lovely tail. The horse ran down to the water and to its delight saw the camel still standing there. Using the same story as the deer, the horse persuaded the camel to part with its tail.

The next morning, the camel went to the water's edge again to look for the deer and the horse and get back its possessions. But of course, they did not appear. To this day, when the camel has a drink, it will take a few sips, then look up and gaze out at the steppes, hoping to catch sight of the deer and the horse, but it never does.

Mongolians use the word genin *(GEN-in) to describe the camel and the same word to describe a person who is too generous for his or her own good.*

TRADITIONAL STORIES

The telling of folktales is an old and important tradition. Besides the entertainment it provides, folktales transmit traditions and values from one generation to the next. Storytellers are usually older people, but there are also professional storytellers who tell stories for money, food, and shelter, often accompanying their stories with songs.

Many folktales feature animals with human qualities as the main characters. The snake is often a bad character, and so is the hedgehog, although it is not as bad as the snake. The lion, the dragon, the elephant, and the mythical *garuda* (ga-ROO-da)—a creature, part-eagle and part-man, who guards a sacred mountain—are strong animals with good attributes. The horse is often magical and intelligent, capable of incredible feats, including flying. Although a man may seem to be the hero in a story, it is the horse that often steals the limelight as the real hero, giving the rider advice, warning of dangers, and foretelling of events to come. The camel is thought of as kind and generous and often too trusting of others.

Some stories depict ordinary, simple folk, with qualities such as honesty, wisdom, and kindness, who triumph over evil, greed, and injustice of all kinds. They include favorite characters such as the clever Badarchin, a wandering lama; the storyteller Dalan Hudalch; and the witty Tsartsan Namjil.

INTERNET LINKS

https://www.amnh.org/explore/science-bulletins/bio/documentaries/the-last-wild-horse-the-return-of-takhi-to-mongolia/article-the-horse-in-mongolian-culture

This article from the American Museum of Natural History discusses the role of horses in Mongolian culture.

https://orgilproductions.com/2016/10/11/popular-sports-in-mongolia

Popular and traditional sports enjoyed in Mongolia are explored on this website.

FESTIVALS

An eagle and its trainer compete at the Golden Eagle Festival.

12

MONGOLIANS CELEBRATE MANY festivals that recognize the ancient culture of their country. Through these celebrations, they give thanks for the bounties of the previous year and for the possibilities of the coming year. However, during the communist era, the state sought to stamp out any religious significance to these holidays. Instead, they became celebrations of the state's objectives, such as the solidarity of workers. Two traditional festivals that survived this era are Tsagaan Sar, which celebrates the first day of the lunar new year, and the national holiday of Naadam. The largest and most popular of Mongolia's festivals, Naadam is observed in July. Other important and festive events are the Khovsgol Ice Festival, the Nauryz (Spring) Festival, and the Golden Eagle Festival.

"I will show you how to call it (the eagle) from the rocks. (It's) probably the most important part of the festival. The judges look at horse riding style, eagle's landing, and eagle flying style. The process is timed and every second counts."

—*The Eagle Huntress*, 2016

THE LUNAR YEAR

Each year in the twelve-year lunar cycle is named for an animal, beginning with the year of the rat, followed by those of the ox, tiger, rabbit, dragon, snake, horse, sheep or goat, monkey, cockerel, dog, and pig. Years have alternating male and female characteristics. The male (called "hard" years) are the rat, tiger, dragon, horse, monkey, and dog years. The rest are female, or "easy," years.

This traditional Kazakh dish of fried dough is often enjoyed during festivals.

CELEBRATING THE NEW YEAR

The exact day for the start of a new year depends on the lunar calendar, but it usually falls between the end of January and early February. New Year's Day is known as "White Moon" or "White Month."

Traditionally, on New Year's Eve, the family gathers at the home of the oldest member for a celebratory meal. On New Year's Day, milk and airag are offered to the spirit of the sky, and each family member has to walk in the direction specified by a book of omens. Finally, family members greet each other with good wishes. The oldest member of the family is the first to be greeted. Once the greetings have been exchanged, the rest of the day is spent in eating, drinking, and socializing. A festive table is usually set up in each home. People go from house to house visiting family and friends.

Activities such as horse races, wrestling, and other competitions are organized by local community leaders as part of the New Year celebrations.

A BIG FESTIVAL

Naadam is the best-known festival and biggest event of the year. It marks the high point of the summer. People travel hundreds of miles across the country to various previously announced meeting grounds, where they can celebrate with sports, games, and feasting. Since 1922, the biggest Naadam has occurred in the capital city, Ulaanbaatar, to celebrate Mongolia's National Day.

For days before the big Naadam, people ride in on their horses—families in trucks and on horse-drawn wooden carts—and set up their gers just outside

THE GOLDEN EAGLE FESTIVAL

Held in October, this annual festival celebrates the centuries-old heritage and traditions of the eagle hunters of western Mongolia. In the Altai Mountains, the hunters and their trained eagles compete in contests that showcase the skills of both trainer and bird. The eagles race to catch small game such as foxes and rabbits. They are judged on accuracy, agility, and speed. The event helps to recognize and preserve the ancient ways of hunting by the Kazakh nomads.

the city. The thick smell of cooking smoke hangs over the encampment. The makeshift town grows as people gather and wait for the entertainment and festivities to begin with a colorful opening ceremony featuring marchers and music in the national stadium.

An archery competition takes place during Naadam.

Naadam is a sports-oriented festival, and the most exciting events are the contests in wrestling, archery, and horse riding. Hundreds of wrestlers come from all over the country to test their strength and skill against each other. The wrestling contests take place in the national stadium. There are no weight categories or age limits as in international wrestling competitions, but the wrestlers are usually big and muscular men. Traditionally, several hundred wrestlers take part in the contest, which lasts throughout the two or three days of the Naadam festival.

Participants in horse riding are seven- to twelve-year-old boys and girls. Races are run over courses from 10 to 20 miles (16 to 32 km). The distance is set by the horse's age, not the child's. The children often ride bareback, already

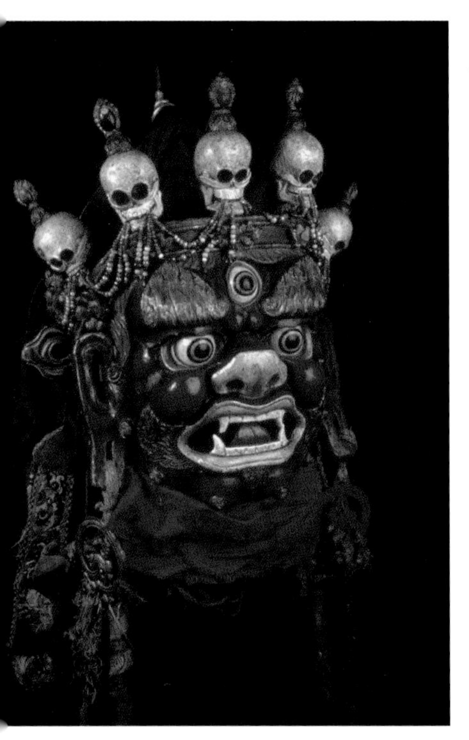

This nineteenth-century mask would be used during Tsam.

being skilled riders and tacticians who have trained for the event. They know how to conserve the horse's energy to go the distance and to find that extra spurt near the finish line. Before the race begins, the young riders pace three times around the starting point in the stadium, giving an ancient war cry. They wear bright and colorful clothes with symbols of good luck on their backs. The course itself takes them once around the stadium, then out into the country where they have to negotiate numerous obstacles such as rivers and hills.

The winning riders do laps of honor around the stadium and canter up to the grandstand to receive the ceremonial bowls of airag, of which they drink a little, pouring the rest on the horses. Honor is also paid to the less fortunate losers. They are led up to the grandstand together with their mounts, while the spectators shout words of encouragement and appreciation for their efforts, and a special chant is said in their honor.

Archery, though called a "manly" sport, has women participants too. The archers are dressed in traditional del and pointed hats. Both men and women use the same kind of bow and shooting technique. When a target is hit, a group of judges sings out a short ceremonial song of praise. The winner of the archery contest is declared "sharpshooter."

A RELIGIOUS FESTIVAL

The religious masked dance festival called Tsam was performed in big Buddhist monasteries in ancient times. It originated in India and spread to Tibet. From there, it was taken to Mongolia in the sixteenth century. Part dance and part mystery play, the masked dance was based on Buddhist mythology, forming part of Buddhist rites. The masks were made from papier-mâché and decorated with precious stones, metals, and coral. They were vividly colored in red, black, yellow, white, and blue, and were bigger than life size so they could be seen clearly and appreciated by the audience. The masks depicted Buddhist deities such as the fierce protector gods and Yama, or Tshoijoo, the Lord of Death. The Mongolian costumes, masks, and sets were different from those in Tibet.

The dances frequently described the triumph of good over evil, with characters such as the funny White Old Man, a buffoon, the Dark Old Man in his black mask and white fangs, and Garuda, the mountain god. These were elements of witchcraft and shamanism.

From the sixteenth to the nineteenth centuries, each of the seven hundred major monasteries staged a big performance, also called Tsam, once a year. The last Tsam was held in Ulaanbaatar in the late 1930s. After that, the communist suppression of Buddhism banned such traditions. There is a reawakening of interest in and celebration of the dance, with older monks teaching younger ones the steps and rituals.

"Mongolian Naadam is inseparably connected to the nomadic civilization of the Mongols, who have long practiced pastoralism on Central Asia's vast steppe." —UNESCO

A CHILD'S FIRST HAIRCUT

The haircutting ceremony occurs when a child is three to five years old and is believed to have survived the dangers of infancy. It is an old nomadic tradition that is celebrated with great joy. Haircutting normally takes place in the fall. Traditionally the day is chosen by a lama. Days beforehand, the preparation of celebratory dishes begins, and on the big day the festive table is laden with food and drink.

The child goes from guest to guest with a pair of scissors and a ceremonial blue silk bag. Each person cuts off a little lock of hair, puts it in the bag, and gives the child a present or gift of money. Throughout the ceremony everyone merrily eats, drinks, and talks.

INTERNET LINKS

http://www.xinhuanet.com/english/2018-02/15/c_136978092.htm
This article focuses on how Mongolians prepare to celebrate the Lunar New Year.

https://www.youtube.com/watch?v=6eJpgo0Jlpg
Videos of traditional to modern festivals are included in "Top 10 Biggest Festivals in Mongolia."

FOOD

A Mongolian family shares a communal meal in their ger.

13

THE MAIN FOODS EATEN IN Mongolia are meat, usually fatty, and dairy products. These are both readily available from the domestic animals that Mongolians raise like camels, cattle, goats, and sheep. Mongolians eat three regular meals a day. Breakfast and lunch usually consist of dairy foods and sometimes meat. The evening meal usually includes meat such as boiled lamb, a favorite dish. Very little seasoning is used except for salt. The whole family gathers for a typical dinner of meat, noodle soup, and tea. Tea is also consumed throughout the day. What eating utensils are used depends on the food served. Chopsticks are used for noodles, spoons for rice and vegetables, and knives for cutting meat.

"Included meals (while visiting Mongolia)? *Boordog* (barbecued marmot), *khorkhog* (barbecued goat), *suutei tsai* (milk tea) and a lot of airag (mare's milk)."

—*Eternal Landscapes: Blogging from the Wild in Mongolia*

A MOSTLY MEAT DIET

Mongolians enjoy beef and lamb, especially the latter. Very little of the sheep is wasted. Besides the meat, the lungs, heart, stomach, intestines, liver, and blood are boiled and eaten. Horsemeat is popular among the Kazakhs in the west. Besides the meat of their domestic animals, Mongolians also like eating marmots, rabbit, deer, and wild boar. Meat that cannot be used soon is dried and preserved. Fish and chicken are not common foods in the Mongolian diet.

Lamb is often prepared by cutting it into joints and smaller pieces, then boiling it or making it into a stew. *Buuz* (BUHZ), a national dish, is a dumpling filled with chopped lamb. *Khuurshuur* (KHER-sher) is a fried pancake made of flour and lamb. Sheep's blood and intestines are the chief ingredients of a sausage-like dish. Barbecued lamb is called *shorlog* (SHOR-log). *Khorkhog* (KHOR-kohg) is usually cooked on special occasions such as festivals. A goat or sheep is killed, dressed, and placed on hot coals, then hot rocks are put inside the carcass so that it is cooked evenly from the inside out.

A dish of fatty meat is prepared in a ger.

Animal fat is relished. Chunks of fat often float in the stews. The Mongolian fat-tailed sheep, a special breed, has a tail that is usually cooked as a delicacy. It is so fatty that it weighs more than 20 pounds (9 kg).

Onions, potatoes, and cabbage have made it into the diet more recently. People in the countryside, especially the less affluent, eat mainly pickled vegetables rather than fresh vegetables and fruit. The short growing season makes the cultivation of vegetables quite difficult. Vegetable farming was left to the Chinese, and that was only after the 1921 revolution when the government introduced farming into the economy.

A staple food for Mongolians is a soft pastry, rolled out and formed into shapes, then deep-fried. Large amounts of this are eaten at mealtimes with meat, cheeses, and tea. Rice, noodles, and bread are also staples.

In more recent times, there has been an increase in the availability of imported food, particularly in the capital, Ulaanbaatar. Western-style supermarkets have appeared and compete with the more traditional Mongolian market stalls. There are many restaurants, bakeries, and tea shops whose customers tend to be among the more well-to-do in local society. Mongolian, Western, and Asian cuisines can all be found in these eateries. The American hot dog is a popular alternative to the lamb sausage.

"Mongolians, we quickly learned, love meat and fat, and in fact consider meat without fat unappetizing and inadequate. Once, when we were trying to buy meat ... a young man we knew brought us a leg of mutton but refused payment because he said the meat wasn't good quality. It was lean, and taking money would be like cheating us."
—M. C. Goldstein and C. M. Beal, *The Changing World of Mongolia's Nomads*

MILK PRODUCTS

Dairy products from camels, mares, sheep, goats, and cows are called "white food" and are second only to meat as the most important food.

The milk is boiled and the skin that forms on the surface is skimmed off and dried slightly to make a soft, creamy, pancake-like food. This is considered a delicacy that is eaten on its own or spread on pastries. To make *arkhi* (AHR-khee), an alcoholic drink, boiled cow's milk is put into a leather bag—standard household equipment found in every ger—and left to ferment. It is stirred with a long wooden paddle every day, churning the milk into butter, which is removed and eaten. The remaining buttermilk is used for the arkhi. All dairy products are made in the summer and fall. Curds from coagulated milk and various cheeses are dried and keep well for months, and are thus always

BORTS

Borts *is a traditional Mongolian dish of air-dried meat, usually beef or goat. For thousands of years, borts has been a staple of nomadic cuisine. The dry climate coupled with the nomadic lifestyle brought about this specific method of preserving meat. Typically, borts is prepared as a winter food, but herders also eat it in summer to avoid slaughtering animals in the heat. Borts is prepared by cutting fresh meat into thin, long strips which are hung on rods to dry, first in a ger for a week and then in a cooler and protected place. When dried, the meat is stored in linen bags that allow air to pass through. Mongol warriors carried borts in linen bags to energize them as they expanded the empire. The meat is said to have healing effects and nutritional benefits. The finished product is best eaten a year after preparation. It appears dark, dry, and shriveled, and has a unique flavor and aroma. It has a chewy texture and can be eaten as is or chopped and added to stews and soups. Some people also add ground borts to milk tea. Even modern city dwellers have a taste for borts, and it is available as a processed food sold in paper bags.*

available for food during the winter months. Despite consuming huge quantities of dairy products and animal fat, studies have not discovered any unusually high levels of cholesterol among the population, possibly because of the heavy physical work of the nomads.

A POT OF TEA

Mongolians drink tea at meals and in between. There is usually a big pot of milk tea in the ger always ready. Milk tea is made by boiling tea leaves in water and adding some milk, butter, and salt gradually to the mixture. It is stirred by scooping it with a ladle and pouring it back into the pot from some height. Sometimes when milk is not available, herders make the tea with salted water, letting it boil for a while.

Milk tea is a common drink of the nomads.

INTERNET LINKS

www.flavorverse.com/traditional-mongolian-foods
Twelve signature foods of Mongolia are featured on this blog, including descriptions of how they taste.

https:/www.worldtravelguide.net/guides/asia/Mongolia/food-and-drink
Mongolian food and drink are explained on this travel guide.

https://www.youtube.com/watch?v=cJBK2J9O2ao
A video guide to traditional Mongolian foods.

GURILTAI SHUL

This is a hearty soup made with meat or borts (dried meat), vegetables, and fried noodles. The amounts and types of meat, vegetables, and spices can vary.

⅔ cup (150 grams) vegetables cut into small pieces
1 onion cut into strips
½ pound (225 g) meat or borts cut into small strips
2 cups (300 g) *tasalsan guril* or fried noodles
Water
Salt, pepper, and other spices

Sauté the onion strips in a pot with a little oil over medium heat.

Add the vegetables and keep frying until browned.

Add the meat and continue frying until the meat is cooked.

Season the meat and vegetables with salt and pepper.

Add enough water to the pot to cover the meat and vegetable mix and turn up the heat until it boils.

Add noodles to the pot and boil for another five minutes.

Season to taste and serve hot.

GAMBIR

These Mongolian pancakes can be made from scratch or from leftover dough. They can be served plain or with jam or jelly on top and eaten with fingers.

2 cups (250 g) flour
½ cup (125 milliliters) water
4 tablespoons sugar
Oil or melted butter

Mix the flour and water to create a pliable dough and let rest for fifteen minutes.

Split the dough into three or four parts to work with individually.

Roll one part into a thin sheet.

Pour a little oil or melted butter onto the sheet, spreading it in all directions.

Sprinkle a little sugar over the surface.

Wrap up the sheet into a long roll.

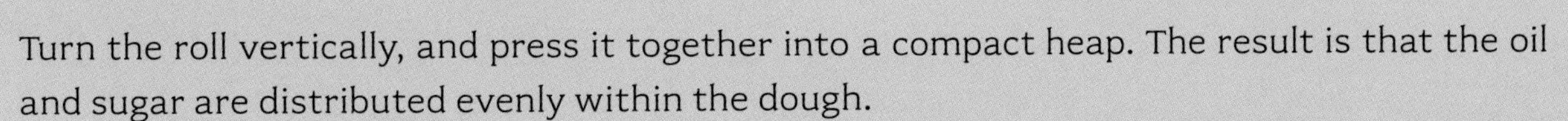

Turn the roll vertically, and press it together into a compact heap. The result is that the oil and sugar are distributed evenly within the dough.

Flatten it again with the rolling pin to a size that will fit in a frying pan.

With a knife, make parallel cuts near the center of the dough to avoid blisters when frying.

Fry the dough in oil or butter on both sides at moderate heat. Fry slowly to cook evenly.

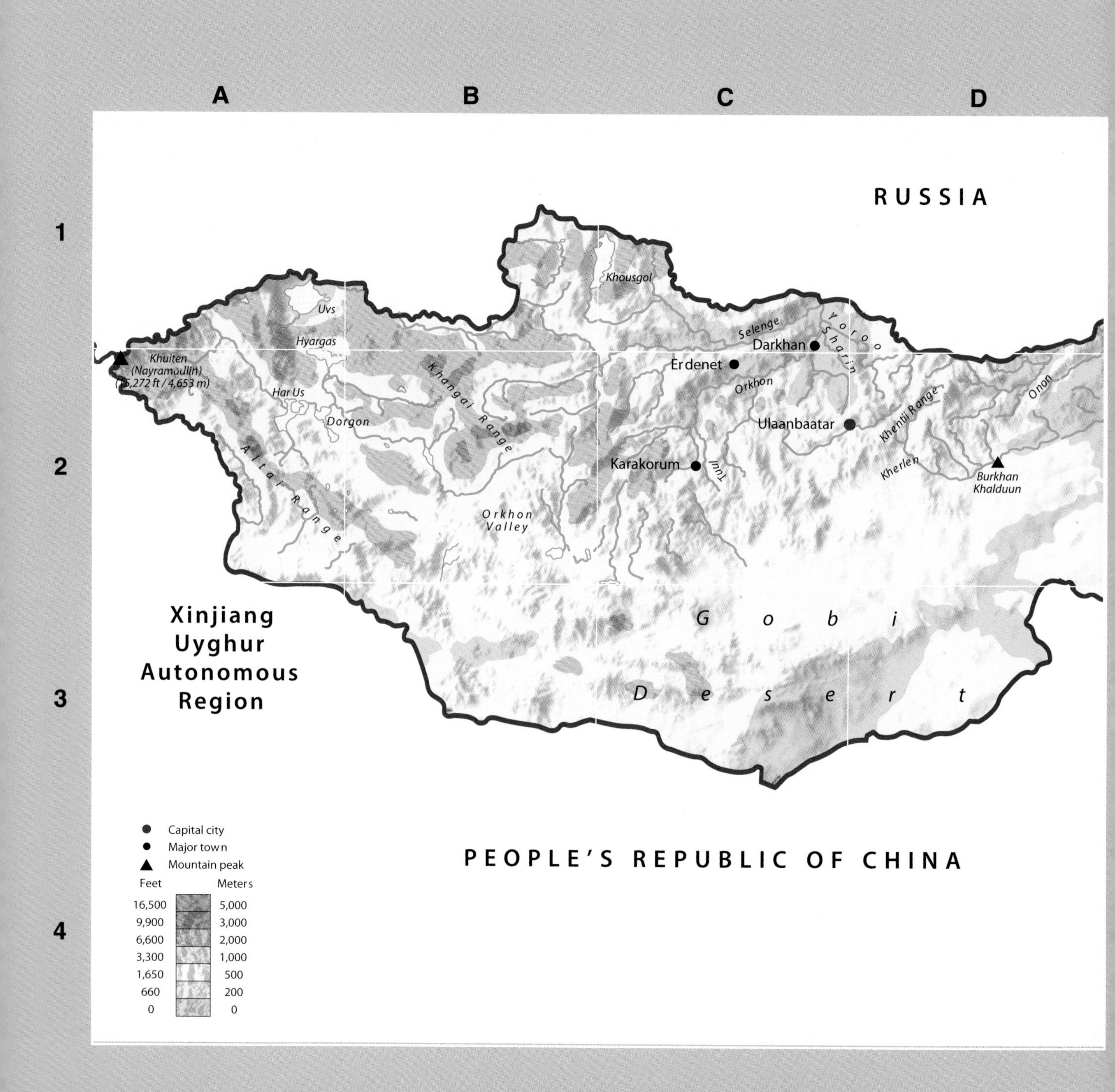
A
B
C
D
1
2
3
4
RUSSIA
Khousgol
Uvs
Hyargas
Selenge
Yoroo
Sharin
Darkhan
Erdenet
Khuiten
(Nayramadlin)
(15,272 ft / 4,653 m)
Har Us
Dorgon
Khangai Range
Orkhon
Ulaanbaatar
Khentii Range
Onon
Karakorum
Tuul
Kherlen
Burkhan
Khalduun
Altai Range
Orkhon
Valley
Xinjiang
Uyghur
Autonomous
Region
Gobi
Desert
Capital city
Major town
Mountain peak
Feet
Meters
16,500
5,000
9,900
3,000
6,600
2,000
3,300
1,000
1,650
500
660
200
0
0
PEOPLE'S REPUBLIC OF CHINA

MAP OF MONGOLIA

E

N

Altai Range, A2

Burkhan Khalduun Mountain, D2

Darkhan, C1

Erdenet, C2

Gobi Desert, B3, C3, D3

Karakorum, C2

Khangai Mountain Range, B2

Khentii Mountain Range, D2

Kherlen River, D2

Khuiten Mountain, A2

Lake Dorgon, A2, B2

Lake Hyargas, A1—A2

Lake Khar Us, A2

Lake Khovsgol, B1, C1

Lake Uvs, A1

Onon River, D1—D2

Orkhon River, C2

Orkhon Valley, B2

People's Republic of China, B3—B4, C3—C4, D3—D4, E1—E4

Russia, A1, B1, C1, D1, E1

Selenge River, C1

Sharin River, C1—C2

Tuul River, C2

Ulaanbaatar, C2, D2

Xinjiang Uyghur Autonomous Region, A2—A4

Yoroo River, C1, D1

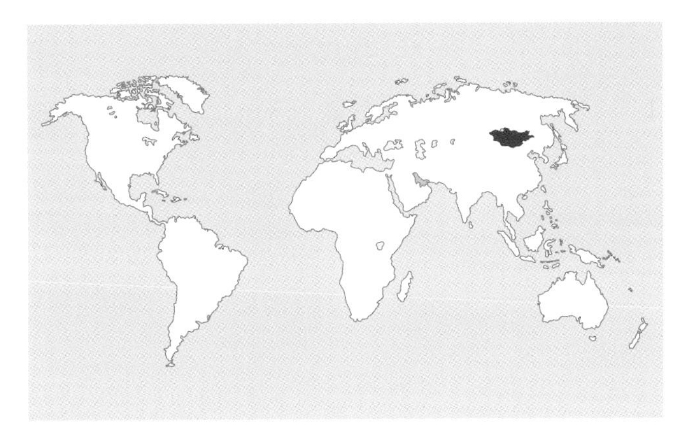

ECONOMIC MONGOLIA

Natural Resources

 Coal

 Copper

 Fluorine

 Gold

 Phosphorus

 Salt

 Timber

 Tin

Services

 Airport

 Tourism

Agriculture

 Camels

 Livestock

Manufacturing

 Textiles

ABOUT THE ECONOMY

OVERVIEW

Mongolia's economy has taken many dramatic swings since the demise of communism in 1990. The termination of Soviet financial assistance saw the gross domestic product (GDP) drop by one-third almost overnight. Then the switch to a freer market economy set in motion a rapid and dramatic growth. Then, in the face of the global financial tumult of 2008 to 2009, the economy declined again. A 10 percent per year growth occurred for the years between 2011 and 2013 because of strong commodity exports and large government spending. In 2017, Mongolia received $5.5 billion from the International Monetary Fund (IMF), which is expected to aid the country's economic and fiscal stability in the long run. As part of the agreement with the IMF, Mongolia is to reform its banking sector. Overall, Mongolia's economy is predicted to move toward increased prosperity as the nation expands its international trade presence.

CURRENCY

Mongolian tugrik (MNT)
1 tugrik (MNT) = 100 mongo
US$1 = 2,378.1 MNT (2017)

GROSS DOMESTIC PRODUCT (GDP)

$38.4 billion (2017 estimate)

GDP PER CAPITA

$12,600 (2017 estimate)

LABOR FORCE

1.24 million (2016 estimate)

LABOR FORCE BY TYPE OF JOB

Agriculture: 31.1 percent
Industry: 18.5 percent
Services: 50.5 percent (2016 estimate)

UNEMPLOYMENT RATE

8 percent (2017 estimate)

INFLATION RATE

4.4 percent (2017 estimate)

MAIN INDUSTRIES

Agriculture; mining (coal, copper, molybdenum, fluorspar, tin, tungsten, and gold); construction and construction materials; oil; food and beverages; processing of animal products, cashmere and natural fiber manufacturing

MAIN EXPORTS

Copper, apparel, livestock, animal products, cashmere, wool, hides, fluorspar, other nonferrous metals, coal, crude oil

MAIN IMPORTS

Machinery and equipment, fuel, cars, food products, industrial consumer goods, chemicals, building materials, sugar, tea, cigarettes and tobacco, appliances, soap and detergent

CULTURAL MONGOLIA

Uvs Nuur Basin
Designated a UNSECO World Heritage Site in 2003, the basin, which is shared with Russia, contains a large, shallow, and highly saline lake. The basin is made up of a dozen protected areas and supports a wide range of birds and other animals, including the endangered snow leopard and a number of rare species of gerbil, jerboas, and the marbled polecat.

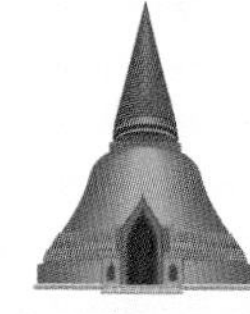

Amarbayasgalant Monastery
Situated in Selenge aimag, it is one of the three most important Buddhist monasteries in Mongolia. Originally built between 1726 and 1736 by the Manchu emperor Yongzheng, the monastery contains the mummified body of the sculptor and painter Zanabazar.

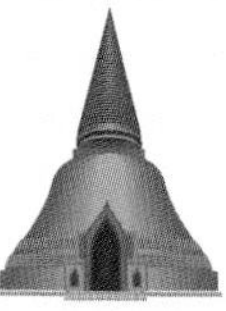

Gandan Monastery
Located in Ulaanbaatar, Gandan is the only monastery to survive the communist purges of the 1930s and 1940s. Also called Gandantegchinlin, it is the biggest and most important monastery in Mongolia. It has been the main center of Buddhist learning in the country since it was established in 1835. Although closed by the communists in 1938, Gandan was allowed to reopen in 1944 and operate under a minimal staff. There are now eight hundred monks at the monastery.

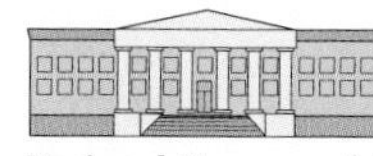

National Museum of Mongolia
Located in the capital city of Ulaanbaatar, the National Museum is one of the main museums in Mongolia. Established in 1991 at the site of the old Museum of the Revolution, the museum is dedicated to preserving Mongolian culture and is involved in scientific and educational pursuits in the areas of historical, archaeological, and ethnographic studies.

Orkhon Valley
Located approximately 218 miles (350 km) west of Ulaanbaatar, the valley was designated a UNESCO World Heritage Site in 2004. It is the locale of a number of historical places that document the development of nomadic pastoral traditions in the area over a span of more than two thousand years. The Orkhon Valley was at the heart of the Mongol Empire.

Erdene Zuu Monastery
Built in 1585, it is thought to be the oldest Buddhist monastery in Mongolia. It was damaged by warfare in the 1680s, rebuilt in the mid-eighteenth century, and then mostly destroyed in the antireligious communist purges of 1939. Only three small temples and the external wall were left standing. It has now been restored as an active monastery as well as a museum open to the public. Erdene Zuu is a part of the Orkhon Valley.

Mongolian National Modern Art Gallery
This museum exhibits contemporary and modern works of Mongolian art that showcase the development of the nation's cultural, historical, and social progress.

Burkhan Khalduun Mountain
Classified as a protected area in 1992, the mountain was originally designated as sacred by Genghis Khan and is considered to be the most sacred mountain in Mongolia. It is part of the Khentii Mountains and is located in Khentii aimag. It is also widely believed to be both the birthplace and the site of the tomb of Genghis Khan.

ABOUT THE CULTURE

OFFICIAL NAME
Mongolia

LAND AREA
599,831 square miles (1,553,556 sq km)

CAPITAL
Ulaanbaatar

MAJOR CITIES
Ulaanbaatar, Erdenet, Darkhan, Khovd, Olgii, Ulaangom

PROVINCES (AIMAGS OR AYMAGS)
One municipality (Ulaanbaatar) plus twenty-one aimags: Arkhangai, Bayankhongor, Bayan-Olgi, Bulgan, Darkhan-Uul, Dornod, Dornogovi, Dundgovi, Govi-Altai, Govisumber, Khentii, Khovd, Khovsgol, Omnogovi, Orkhon, Ovorkhangai, Selenge, Sukhbaatar, Tov, Uvs, Zavkhan

HIGHEST POINT
Nayramadlin Orgil (Khuiten Peak) (14,350 feet/4,374 m)

MAJOR WATERWAYS
Lake Khovsgol, Lake Uvs, Lake Khar Us, Selenge River, Orkhon River, Kherlen River

POPULATION
3,068,243 (2018 estimate)

LIFE EXPECTANCY
Total population: 69.9 years
Male: 65.7 years
Female: 74.4 years (2018 estimate)

BIRTHRATE
2.09 children born per female (2017)

ETHNIC GROUPS
Khalkha, 81.9 percent; Kazakh, 3.8 percent; Dorvod, 2.7 percent; Bayad, 2.1 percent; Buryat, 1.7 percent; Zakhchin, 1.2 percent; Dariganga, 1 percent; Uriankhai, 1 percent; other (including Chinese and Russian), 4.6 percent (2010 estimate)

LITERACY RATE
98.4 percent of the population over age fifteen can read and write
Male, 98.2 percent; female, 98.6 percent (2015 estimate)

RELIGION
Buddhist Lamaist, 53 percent; Muslim, 3 percent; Shamanist, 2.9 percent; Christian, 2.2 percent; other, 0.4 percent; none, 38.6 percent (2010 estimate)

LANGUAGES
Mongolian (Khalkha dialect), 95 percent; Turkic and Russian, 5 percent (2017)

TIMELINE

IN MONGOLIA	IN THE WORLD
2nd–1st centuries BCE Nomadic peoples move farther west near China.	**116–117 CE** The Roman Empire reaches its greatest extent, under Emperor Trajan (98–117 CE).
317 CE Xianbei conquer northern China.	
1196–1206 Temujin unifies the Mongols and assumes the title of Genghis (Chinggis) Khan.	
1206–1215 Genghis expands the Mongolian Empire south to Beijing and west to Lake Balkash.	**1215** The Magna Carta is signed.
1220–1226 Most of southwest Asia is conquered, and Europe and China are invaded.	
1227 Genghis dies during the siege of Hsingchungfu. His son Ogedei becomes Khan.	
1237–1241 The invasion of Europe ends at Vienna with the death of Ogedei.	
1261 Kublai is made Great Khan.	
1391 Timur defeats the Golden Horde.	
1400–1454 The Mongol Empire crumbles under civil war.	**1530** Beginning of transatlantic slave trade organized by the Portuguese in Africa.
1586 Buddhism becomes the main religion.	
1636 Inner Mongolia is created.	
1691 Outer Mongolia is created.	
1911 The Qing dynasty falls. Outer Mongolia declares independence.	**1914** World War I begins.
1919 Occupation by Chinese army	
1920 The Mongolian People's Party (MPP) is formed.	**1939** World War II begins.

IN MONGOLIA	IN THE WORLD
1924 The birth of the Mongolian People's Republic.	
1945 Mongolians vote for independence in a UN plebiscite.	**1945** World War II ends.
1952 Prime Minister Khorloogiin Choibalsan dies and is replaced by Yumjaagiin Tsedenbal.	
1965 Tsedenbal purges the intelligentsia.	**1966** The Chinese Cultural Revolution
1984 Tsedenbal resigns and the Mongolian Democratic Association is formed.	**1986** Nuclear power disaster at Chernobyl in Ukraine.
1990 First democratic elections are held; the MPRP wins.	**1991** Breakup of the Soviet Union.
1993 The first direct presidential election is held and won by the opposition candidate Punsalmaagiin Ochirbat.	
1996 The opposition wins elections and forms the first noncommunist government.	**1997** Hong Kong is returned to China.
2001 The IMF grants a $40 million loan to address poverty and increase economic growth.	**2001** Terrorists crash planes into New York, Washington, DC, and Pennsylvania.
2004 MPRP forms a coalition government headed by Tsakhiagiin Elbegdorj.	**2005** Hurricane Katrina devastates the Louisiana, Mississippi, and Alabama coasts.
2006 Coalition government is dissolved by MPRP; new coalition is formed by Miyeegombyn Enkhbold.	**2016** United Kingdom withdraws from the EU.
2017 The IMF and other partners award Mongolia $5.5 billion; Khaltmaa Battulga is elected president.	**2017** United States withdraws from the Paris Climate Agreement.
2018 Activities of the Mongolian Financial Regulatory Commission (FRC) are examined after complaints.	**2018** Nuclear and missile tests are suspended in North Korea.

GLOSSARY

aimag **or *aymag* (AI-mug)**
A province or political subdivision, like states, of which there are twenty-one in Mongolia.

airag **(AI-rug)**
Fermented mare's milk.

arkhi **(AHR-khee)**
Alcoholic drink distilled from cow's milk.

bielgee **(BEE-el-gee)**
Mongolian dance performed solo by a girl.

del **(DEHL)**
Traditional Mongolian outer garment worn by both men and women.

ger **(GUHR)**
Portable tent dwelling made of felt. Also called a yurt.

Khalkha (HAL-ha)
A traditionally nomadic people living in eastern and central Mongolia. The name means "shield" or "alliance."

khoomi **(KHAW-me)**
Throat singing.

lama
Buddhist monk.

morin khuur **(MAW-rin kher)**
Two-stringed Mongolian fiddle with a head shaped like a horse's head.

ortoo **(OOR-taw)**
Relay station for the courier system of horse riders.

ovoo **(AW-waw)**
A rustic shrine constructed from mounds of rocks to honor various gods and spirits.

shudrag **(SHOOD-rug)**
Three-stringed Mongolian lute.

Silk Road
An ancient trade route linking China and imperial Rome, named for the silk transported on it. Caravans generally met on the road and traded goods and news.

Soyombo (SOH-yom-bo)
Mongolian symbol on the national flag consisting of a flame, a sun, a crescent moon, two intertwined fish (yin-yang), rectangles, and triangles.

State Great Hural
The Mongolian one-house parliament.

Tengri (TENG-ri)
The supreme or eternal sky god.

tugrik
Mongolian currency.

yoching **(YAW-ching)**
Mongolian zither with metal strings stretched on a board, played by striking with two hammers.

zurag **(ZOO-rug)**
A two-dimensional painting style in Mongolia that uses distinctive colors and depicts the traditional lifestyle.

FOR FURTHER INFORMATION

BOOKS

Bjorklund, Ruth. *Mongolia: Enchantment of the World*. New York: Scholastic, 2016.

Bodio, Stephen J. *Eagle Dreams: Searching for Legends in Wild Mongolia*. New York: Skyhorse Publishing, 2015.

Gray, Susan H. *Mongolian Wild Horse*. North Mankato, MN: Cherry Lake Publishing, 2014.

Joo, Mi-hwa. *Where the Winds Meet*. New York: Lerner Publications, 2015.

Lewin, Ted, and Betsy Lewin. *Horse Song: The Naadam of Mongolia*. New York: Lee and Low Books, 2008.

Reynolds, Jan. *Mongolia*. Vanishing Cultures. New York: Lee and Low Books, 2007.

Robinson, Carl. *Mongolia: Nomad Empire of Eternal Blue Sky*. Hong Kong: Odyssey Publications, 2010.

Tschinag, Galsan. *The Blue Sky*. Minneapolis, MN: Milkweed Editions, 2007.

Waugh, Louise. *Hearing Birds Fly: A Nomadic Year in Mongolia*. London, UK: Little, Brown Book Group, 2003.

FILMS

Bell, Otto. *The Eagle Huntress*. Kissaki Films and Stacey Reiss Productions, 2016.

Pilot Film & TV Productions. *Globe Trekker: Mongolia*. 2010

Rufo, Christopher. *Roughing It: Mongolia*. PBS, 2017.

Soederhamn, Martin. *A Journey Through Mongolia*. Adventure Calls, 2017.

MUSIC

Jonon: Mongolian National Music Band. *The Grace of the Khaans*. Orange Records, 2016.

Various artists. *Mongolia—Living Music of the Steppes*. Music of the Earth, 2009.

Various artists. *Mongolia: Traditional Music*. Smithsonian Folkways Music, 2014.

BIBLIOGRAPHY

BOOKS

Badarch, Dendevin, Raymond A. Zilinskas, and Peter J. Balint, eds. *Mongolia Today: Science, Culture, Environment and Development*. New York: Routledge, 2015.

Becker, Jasper. *Mongolia: Travels in an Untamed Land*. London, UK: Legend Press, 2015.

Christian, David. *A History of Russia, Central Asia and Mongolia*. Hoboken, NJ: Wiley-Blackwell, 2018.

Gupta, Gauri Shankar. *Mongolia: The Land of Blue Skies*. New Delhi, India: Roli Books, 2008.

McLynn, Frank. *Genghis Khan: His Conquests, His Empire, His Legacy*. Boston: Da Capo Press, 2016.

Morgan, David. *The Mongols*. 2nd ed. Hoboken, NJ: Wiley-Blackwell, 2007.

Severin, Tim. *In Search of Genghis Khan: An Exhilarating Journey on Horseback Across the Steppes of Mongolia*. New York: Cooper Square Press, 2003.

Sexton, Patricia. *Live from Mongolia: From Wall Street Banker to Mongolian News Anchor*. New York: Beaufort Books, 2013.

Soni, Sharad K., ed. *Mongolia Today: Internal Changes and External Linkages*. New Delhi, India: Pentagon Press, 2016.

Turner, Kevin. *Sky Shamans of Mongolia: Meetings with Remarkable Healers*. Berkeley, CA: North Atlantic Books, 2016.

Voss, Peter. *Mongolia*. Petersberg, Germany: Michael Imhof Verlag, 2016.

Weatherford, Jack. *Genghis Khan and the Quest for God*. New York: Penguin Books, 2017.

WEBSITES

All Mongolian Recipes: The Food of the Nomads. https://www.mongolfood.info/en/recipes.

British Broadcasting Corporation: Mongolia Timeline. http://news.bbc.co.uk/2/hi/asia-pacific/1235612.stm.

CIA World Factbook: Mongolia. https://www.cia.gov/library/publications/the-world-factbook/geos/mg.html.

Mongolia Society. http://mongoliasociety.org.

Mongolia Tourist Information Center. http://www.touristinfocenter.mn/en/home.aspx.

National Parks of Mongolia. https://www.worldatlas.com/articles/national-parks-of-mongolia.html.

United States Department of State: US Relations with Mongolia. https://www.state.gov/r/pa/ei/bgn/2779.htm.

WeatherOnline: Mongolia. https://www.weatheronline.co.uk/reports/climate/Mongolia.htm.

World Bank in Mongolia: Overview. http://www.worldbank.org/en/country/mongolia/overview.

INDEX

aimags, 34, 42
airag, 43, 77, 91, 120, 122
Andrews, Roy Chapman, 14, 17, 112
archery, 9, 23, 111–112, 121–122

banking, 49–50, 53
Batmonkh, Jambyn, 30, 35–36
Battulga, Khaltmaa, 31, 37, 39
Batu Khan, 24–25
Bogd Khan, 18, 26–28
boots, 71, 80, 101
Bronze Age, 102

camels, 6, 17, 43, 45–46, 65, 76–78, 112, 115–117, 125, 127
carving, 102, 107
cashmere, 8, 45, 50
chess, 115
China, 5–6, 8, 11, 13, 17–18, 21–30, 33–34, 38–39, 42, 46, 48–50, 69, 86–87, 93–94, 96, 104, 127
Choibalsan, Khorloogiin, 28–30, 38, 87
climate, 14, 16–17, 34, 43, 57, 60, 128
climate change, 58
clothing, 30, 69, 71–73, 77, 107, 114, 122
coal, 18–19, 42, 44–45, 52–53, 60, 69
collectivization, 28, 35, 43, 70–71
communism, 7–9, 21, 27–28, 30, 33, 35, 38, 41–43, 50, 69–71, 85, 87–88, 90–91, 119, 123
construction, 7, 19, 38, 44–46, 83
copper, 18–19, 44, 50, 53
crafts, 24, 87, 101, 105, 107
currency, 49–50

dancing, 109, 112, 122–123
Darkhan, 19, 42, 46, 88
deforestation, 8, 44, 55, 58
democracy, 7, 21, 30–31, 33–39, 43, 91, 96
demonstrations, 31, 33, 35, 37
desertification, 55, 58
diseases, 81
drought, 56, 63

education, 30, 38, 47, 51, 69–71, 75, 79, 81–83, 95–96, 115
Elbegdorj, Tsakhiagiin, 31, 36–37, 67
elections, 30–31, 34, 36–37
endangered species, 12, 17, 61, 63–65
energy, 18, 42, 44–45, 60, 76
Enkhbayar, Nambaryn, 37
Erdenet, 18–19, 42, 45
erosion, 8, 58, 61
exports, 44–45, 47, 50, 53

farming, 18, 41–44, 51, 56–58, 71, 127
felt, 18, 45, 71–72, 77–78, 80
festivals
  Golden Eagle Festival, 119, 121
  Naadam, 9, 112, 119–123
  New Year, 119–120
  Tsam, 122–123
feudalism, 7, 28, 33, 69–70
food, 9, 19, 43–45, 50, 53, 62, 76–77, 79, 111, 123, 125–129
foreign investment, 18, 35, 41, 43, 53
forests, 12, 44, 58, 61–63, 65
fossils, 6, 13–14

Genghis Khan, 5, 9, 21–24, 69, 85–86, 88–89, 94, 96, 104–106, 112
gers (yurts), 6, 18, 47, 52, 76–78, 80, 98, 107, 109, 115, 120–121, 127–129
goats, 8, 15, 43, 45, 62, 76–77, 112, 125–128
Gobi Desert, 6, 13–14, 17, 34, 57, 63, 65
gold, 18, 44, 53, 107
Golden Horde, 25
Great Wall, 22, 25

haircutting ceremony, 89, 123
health, 61, 68, 81
herding, 5, 7, 28, 41–44, 47, 49, 58, 62, 69–71, 76–77, 99, 113, 128
highest point, 12
horses, 5–6, 9, 15, 17–18, 23–24, 43, 46–47, 49, 64–65, 69, 76–78, 80, 90, 94, 107–108, 111–114, 116–117, 120–122, 126
Hulegu Khan, 25
hunting, 23, 44, 52, 62–63, 69, 81, 91, 101, 107, 111, 113, 121

imports, 45, 47, 50, 127
independence, 26–30, 39, 87
inflation, 53
Inner Mongolia, 9, 25–27, 93–94
internet, 48

Japan, 25, 30, 38–39, 50, 108

Karakorum, 24–25, 85, 88, 105
Kublai Khan, 5, 25, 86, 94–95

lakes, 6, 12, 14, 16, 47, 59–60, 90–91, 94, 115
lamas (monks), 26, 28, 70, 79, 86–88, 91, 95, 104–105, 117, 123
languages
  dialects, 69, 93–94
  Kazakh, 95
  Korean, 95
  Mongolian, 25, 86, 88, 93–98, 101, 105
  Russian, 30, 83, 95, 97
  Soyombo, 97
  Tuvan, 95
leather, 23, 49, 60, 71, 77–78, 80, 87, 112, 127
legal system, 34, 90
literacy, 82
literature, 73, 77, 104–105

marriage, 73, 79–80, 89
masks, 122–123
media
  newspapers, 96
  radio, 48, 76, 96–97, 114

INDEX

television, 45, 48, 97–98, 114
military, 38–39
milk, 9, 43, 76–77, 79, 90, 120, 127, 129
mining, 7–8, 18, 42–44, 46, 53, 56, 59–60, 69, 71
monasteries, 8, 28, 42, 69–70, 73, 81, 86–88, 90, 101, 105, 122–123
Mongol Empire, 5, 9, 21–26, 38, 49, 67, 86, 88–89, 94–95, 104–106
mountains, 6, 12, 14, 16–18, 23, 52, 65, 67, 77, 90–91, 115, 121
music, 9, 24, 96–97, 107–109, 111, 114, 121

names, 98
national parks, 52, 63, 65
Natsagdorj, Dashdorjiin, 73, 105, 108
nomads, 5–8, 22, 41–42, 45, 47, 55–56, 63, 68, 71, 76–77, 79, 82–83, 99, 101–102, 105–106, 112–113, 114, 121, 123, 128–129

Ochirbat, Punsalmaagiin, 35–36
Ogedei Khan, 24
Olympic Games, 115
overgrazing, 57–58
ovoo, 91, 102

painting, 73, 87, 101, 103
people
  Dukha, 62
  Kazakhs, 69, 90, 95, 121, 126
  Khalkha Mongols, 26, 68–69, 94
  Tuvinians, 69
  Uyghurs, 22, 69, 86, 94, 103, 105
poetry, 73, 102, 104–106
political parties, 27–31, 35–37, 71, 96
pollution, 8, 55, 58–61, 63
Polo, Marco, 5, 14
population, 6–7, 11, 18–19, 42, 51, 59, 67–69, 90
poverty, 8, 51, 79
privatization, 31, 41, 43, 52–53, 58
Przewalski's horses, 17, 64–65
purges, 28, 35, 87

racing, 9, 111, 112, 120, 121–122
religions
  Buddhism, 8, 18, 26, 28, 69–70, 85–88, 90, 103–105, 122–123
  Christianity, 85, 90
  Islam, 23, 25, 69, 85, 90
  shamanism, 8, 85–86, 88–90, 102, 123
rivers, 6, 16, 18, 47, 59, 67, 91, 105–106, 115, 122
Russia, 5, 7, 11–12, 16, 18, 21, 23–30, 33–35, 38–39, 45, 47–50, 62, 64, 69, 94–97, 108, 114

Secret History of the Mongols, The, 104, 106
Sharav, Balduugiin, 73, 103
sheep, 12, 15, 28, 41, 43, 62, 72, 76–77, 80, 112, 125–127
Silk Road, 22–23
snow leopards, 12, 65, 81
solar power, 45, 77, 98
sports, 111–112, 115, 120–122
Stalin, Joseph, 28
State Great Hural (parliament), 7, 30–31, 34–37
steppes, 6, 15, 17–18, 22, 42, 44, 57–58, 62, 64, 76, 113
storytelling, 101–102, 104, 116–117
Sukhbaatar, Damdiny, 28–29, 38

taiga, 62
tea, 49, 80, 125, 127–129
throat singing (*khoomi*), 108
Tibet, 8, 27, 81, 86–88, 94–95, 104, 122
timber, 42–45, 46, 58
tourism, 7, 12, 52
transportation,
  air travel, 47–48
  railway, 43, 45–47
  roads, 46–47
Tsedenbal, Yumjaagiin, 30, 35

Ulaanbaatar (Urga), 6, 9, 11, 18, 27–29, 31, 34, 42, 44–49, 52, 58, 60, 77, 80–81, 87–88, 97, 108, 115, 120, 123, 127
unemployment, 43, 51, 79
Ungern-Sternberg, Roman von, 27–29

water, 8, 14, 16, 55, 58–60, 76, 81
White Russian army, 27–28, 30, 38
women, 68, 71–73, 75, 77–79, 89, 99, 112, 122
wool, 8, 43, 45, 50, 71, 77, 80
World War I, 27
World War II, 38
wrestling, 9, 98, 111–112, 115, 120–121

yaks, 46, 76–78
Yuan dynasty, 25, 86, 95

Zanabazar, Gombordorji, 26, 87–88, 97, 104